L[...]
FA[...]
IN A
FRAGMENTED
WORLD

Christian Mission and Modern Culture

EDITED BY
ALAN NEELY, H. WAYNE PIPKIN,
AND WILBERT R. SHENK

In the Series:

LIVING
FAITHFULLY
IN A
FRAGMENTED
WORLD

Lessons for the Church from
MacIntyre's After Virtue

JONATHAN R. WILSON

TRINITY PRESS
INTERNATIONAL
HARRISBURG, PENNSYLVANIA

First published by
TRINITY PRESS INTERNATIONAL
P.O. Box 1321
Harrisburg, PA 17105

Trinity Press International is a division of the Morehouse Group.

Scripture quotations are from the New Revised Standard Version Bible, copyright 1989, Division of Christian Education of the National Council of the Churches of Christ in the United States of America, and are used by permission.

Cover design: Brian Preuss

Library of Congress Cataloging-in-Publication Data
Wilson, Jonathan R.
    Living faithfully in a fragmented world : lessons for the church from MacIntyre's After virtue / Jonathan R. Wilson.
        p. cm. — (Christian mission and modern culture series)
    Includes bibliographical references.
    ISBN 1-56338-240-7
    1. Mission of the church. 2. Church and the world.
3. Christian ethics. 4. Culture conflict—Moral and ethical aspects. 5. Culture conflict—United States—History—20th century. 6. United States—Moral conditions. 7. MacIntyre, Alasdair C. After virtue.
I. Title. II. Series: Christian mission and modern culture.
    BV601.8.W49   1998
    241—dc21   97-32871
                                                              CIP

Printed in the United States of America
98 99 00 01 02 6 5 4 3 2 1

Contents

Preface to the Series

Both Christian mission and modern culture, widely regarded as antagonists, are in crisis. The emergence of the modern mission movement in the early nineteenth century cannot be understood apart from the rise of technocratic society. Now, at the end of the twentieth century, both modern culture and Christian mission face an uncertain future.

One of the developments integral to modernity was the way the role of religion in culture was redefined. Whereas religion had played an authoritative role in the culture of Christendom, modern culture was highly critical of religion and increasingly secular in its assumptions. A sustained effort was made to banish religion to the backwaters of modern culture.

The decade of the 1980s witnessed further momentous developments on the geopolitical front with the collapse of communism. In the aftermath of the breakup of the system of power blocs that dominated international relations for a generation, it is clear that religion has survived even if its institutionalization has undergone deep change and its future forms are unclear. Secularism continues to oppose religion, while technology has emerged as a major source of power and authority in modern culture. Both confront Christian faith with fundamental questions.

The purpose of this series is to probe these developments from a variety of angles with a view to helping the church understand its missional responsibility to a culture in crisis. One important resource is the church's experience of two centuries of cross-cultural mission that has reshaped the church into a global Christian *ecumene*. The focus of our inquiry will be the church in modern culture. The series (1) examines modern/postmodern culture from a missional point of view; (2) develops the theological agenda that the church in modern culture must address in order to recover its own integrity; and (3) tests fresh conceptualizations of the nature and mission of the church as it engages modern culture. In other words, these volumes are intended to be a forum where conventional assumptions can be challenged and alternative formulations explored.

This series is a project authorized by the Institute of Mennonite Studies, research agency of the Associated Mennonite Biblical Seminary, and supported by a generous grant from the Pew Charitable Trusts.

Editorial Committee

ALAN NEELY
H. WAYNE PIPKIN
WILBERT R. SHENK

Acknowledgments

Many friends have contributed to this work. I first learned to read MacIntyre from Stanley Hauerwas and Thomas Spragens, Jr., at Duke University. There also, a wonderful group of graduate students contributed to my thinking. Klaus Bockmuehl, now with the Lord, helped me crystallize what I wanted to say about MacIntyre for an essay in *CRUX*, of which he was then the editor. Don Lewis, who succeeded Klaus as editor of *CRUX,* then published the essay (Wilson 1990). That essay prompted Wilbert Shenk to invite me to expand the argument of the essay for this series. I am grateful to him for the invitation. I am also indebted to Philip Rolnick and Thomas Langford for the many thought-provoking questions they raised in response to that essay. Professor MacIntyre kindly read that early essay and corrected some errors and misrepresentations that it contained.

I am indebted to Dean George V. Blankenbaker and the Professional Development Committee of Westmont College for granting me a semester's sabbatical during which I completed this manuscript.

My wife, Marti Crosby, and our daughter, Leah, have been a constant source of encouragement for my writing, but, of more importance, for living faithfully. I owe much to their loving discipline. Finally, I dedicate this book to my father, J. Reford Wilson (1924–1995), and my mother, M. Gene Wilson, who have faithfully given their lives in witness to the gospel.

Introduction

This book is written under the conviction that the church in Western culture is in grave danger of compromising its faithfulness to the gospel. Of course, such conviction is almost always present somewhere in the church. Nevertheless, because of the enormous changes that are taking place in our culture, such conviction takes on greater significance. This book is also written under the conviction that the changes taking place in Western culture present a wonderful opportunity for faithful witness to the gospel, as the church in the West reexamines its own life and witness and discovers once again the power of the gospel of Jesus Christ to redeem humanity.

Guided by these twin convictions, I describe in this book several aspects of contemporary culture that create both opportunities for and threats to Christian mission. On the basis of this description, I suggest some understandings and practices that the church must adopt today in order to live faithfully and witness effectively to the gospel of Jesus Christ.

The call to faithful living and witness is given to the church in the "Great Commission":

And Jesus came and said to them,"All authority in heaven and on earth has been given to me. Go

1

INTRODUCTION

therefore and make disciples of all nations, baptizing them in the name of the Father and of the
Son and of the Holy Spirit, and teaching them to
obey everything that I have commanded you. And
remember, I am with you always, to the end of the
age" (Matt. 28:18–20).

In this passage, Jesus Christ calls the church to particular practices: making disciples, baptizing and teaching
them. In the midst of much discussion about the relationship between these various practices, one thing is
clear: their point of reference is the good news of Jesus
Christ. This good news is an ever-present, unchanging
reality: Jesus himself promises to be with us always. So
the gospel that the church is commissioned to proclaim
is not something we merely conjure up from the past or
hope for in the future, although it certainly has a past
and a future. Rather, the redemption of Jesus Christ is a
present reality that he is actively accomplishing in our
world today. Therefore, the church's responsibility is to
participate in that redemption and witness to it. We are
witnesses to Jesus Christ, ambassadors of God's reconciliation that is being accomplished through Christ. This
responsibility extends to all peoples, to bring the gospel
to them and educate them in the practices of the
gospel—baptizing and teaching—so that they may participate in this redemption and become its witnesses.

This gospel and the mission of the church never
change, but the circumstances in which we witness to
and live out the gospel do change. With changing circumstances comes the need to rethink how the church
lives faithfully and witnesses to the gospel. Changing circumstances bring new opportunities for witness, but

they also bring new threats to the integrity of the church's witness. For example, Christians in some parts of Africa encounter the question of polygamy. Addressing this issue and shaping the life of the church to respond to this question provide opportunities to live out the gospel in that situation, but they also threaten the possibility of unfaithfulness. We have recognized this same truth in situations closer to home. For example, how the church in the West handles the questions of divorce and remarriage is shaped by and shapes our understanding of the gospel. Sometimes the differences are more subtle but are still very significant; for example, we know that a church in suburban Denver and one in downtown Denver face different challenges and look different. In other words, although the unchanging mission of the church is to witness to the good news of Jesus Christ, that witness must always discern the present reality of that redemption and shape the church's mission accordingly.

It is clear that the church faces many threats to its faithfulness. Words are important here. The *gospel* is never threatened by changing circumstances; God's purpose in Jesus Christ is being accomplished and nothing can hinder that. All authority has been given to Jesus Christ. However, what may be compromised is the church's faithfulness to the gospel. Even here, the church may be made a witness to Jesus Christ by God's judgment. That is, even an unfaithful church may be used to witness to the gospel by God's judgment upon it. So what is at issue for us is not the gospel or witness to the gospel, but the church's faithfulness to the commission given by Jesus Christ.

This understanding of the mission of the church must be disciplined by the gospel and firmly grounded

in the conviction that "relevance" is an intrinsic characteristic of the gospel, not a demand of the culture.
Otherwise, the quest for relevance becomes a quest for
acceptance. As Julian Hartt reminds us, there is a great
difference between the church asking the world, "Are
you getting the message?" and asking the world, "Do
you like the message?" or "Will you go on loving me
even if you don't like my message?" (Hartt 1967:345).

Enormous changes are taking place in the culture
within which we are called to witness. Although we
have often been sensitive to changing circumstances—from America to Africa, from suburban
Denver to urban Denver—we have not always been
aware of our own culture's historicity. Or, as I will
later argue, when we have shown some sensitivity to
historical forces, we have often misread that history
or indulged in a misplaced nostalgia. As a result of this
neglect and misreading, the church is unprepared for
the new challenges and opportunities that we face. We
are in danger of failing to communicate the good news
of Jesus Christ or of cloaking a nostalgia for the past
in Christian language and mistaking its acceptance for
acceptance of gospel.

The church is particularly vulnerable in times when
a familiar, and comfortable culture is changing. When a
culture has been regnant for some time (even though
there may be some minor changes along the way), it
becomes familiar, and the church develops strategies for
faithful living and witness in that culture. But those
established strategies may not be helpful in changing
circumstances. Just as antibiotics aid the human body
in resisting and conquering bacterial infections but are
ineffective against viral infections, so also strategies

used by the church for living and witnessing faithfully in one culture may be ineffective in another culture.

At the present time, I believe that the church is in grave danger of compromising the gospel and the integrity of its witness by mistakenly relying on strategies that are not effective in our changing times. My concern is primarily with the church that is situated in Western culture—the culture of Europe and North America. As we move toward a global culture dominated by the technologies and economies of this culture, my concern becomes increasingly global. Nevertheless, the church in Western culture faces particular challenges that arise from the history of its impact on this culture.

In order to be faithful to the unchanging, ever-present Jesus Christ and to the mission given it by Jesus Christ, the church must carefully and persistently attend to its circumstances. We live in a time of tremendous change and uncertainty. In such a time, the church has many opportunities for revitalized witness to the gospel. New ways of living out the gospel arise, and people who thought they had the church and the gospel figured out and written off may have to reconsider its relevance and truth. At the same time, the church's faithfulness to the gospel must be vigorously guarded. As circumstances change, new threats to the truth of the gospel may arise. For example, with religious freedom in Russia and the republics of the former Soviet Union, the church has tremendous opportunities to present the gospel to spiritually hungry people. At the same time, however, the church in those states has had to contend with the rise of religious cults—a problem that did not exist in the USSR and one that the church is ill-prepared to meet.

Because changing circumstances bring new threats, the church must continually discern the characteristics of the particular culture within which it is called to faithfulness. This is true of the church in all times and places. The concern of this book will be the faithfulness of the church in Western culture.

One of the most powerful and far-reaching analyses of Western culture is Alasdair MacIntyre's *After Virtue.*[1] Although MacIntyre's later work grows beyond *After Virtue* in ways that we will consider below, *After Virtue* remains MacIntyre's seminal work and his most incisive analysis of Western culture. In this book, MacIntyre traces the history of Western moral traditions and argues that this history has brought us to a critical time in our culture. Although focused on ethical theory, MacIntyre's account incorporates a compact and incisive analysis of the whole of our society. We are faced, he says, with two paths, which we will explore in the following chapters. We may follow Nietzsche down the path that views morality as simply an expression of emotional preference and social relationships as an arena for the exercise of power. Or we may follow Aristotle down the path that leads to community rooted in the narrative of a tradition and embodied in certain virtues and practices.

MacIntyre's analysis provides some powerful lessons for the church's faithfulness. However, because MacIntyre's "tradition" in this analysis is more Aristotelian than Christian, we will have to make some adjustments as we follow his analysis. Following the writing of *After Virtue*, MacIntyre returned to the church, and his later works, *Whose Justice? Which Rationality?* and *Three Rival Versions of Moral Enquiry*, show the dominance of the

Augustinian-Thomistic tradition in MacIntyre's thought. However, these later works do not display the same incisive analysis of Western culture found in the earlier work and even the turn to Christianity in them is incomplete.[2]

Even though we will have to make some adjustments along the way, *After Virtue* is the text from which we will draw several lessons for the church to live and witness faithfully. The first lesson is the need to attend to our history. Under the influence of modernity, the church has tended to be ahistorical. By telling the story of Western moral traditions, MacIntyre shows us that history constitutes an argument and determines the range of possibilities open to us. Therefore, in the first chapter I tell briefly the history of the church in relation to Western culture as that history determines how the church is to live and witness faithfully today.

In the second chapter, I pursue MacIntyre's suggestion that we live in a fragmented world rather than a pluralistic world. I show the differences between fragmentation and pluralism and its significance for Christian mission. In the third chapter, I summarize MacIntyre's story of the mainstream of morality in Western culture. I show how the church has compromised its faithfulness by accommodating to that mainstream and how many current conceptions of the mission of the church continue that mistake. In the fourth chapter, I summarize MacIntyre's story of the minority, Aristotelian tradition in Western culture. I replace his account with one rooted in the gospel of Jesus Christ and the Christian community. In the fifth chapter, I draw on MacIntyre's suggestion that we need a "new monasticism" in order to consider what forms the life of the church must take to sustain faithful witness in contemporary culture. In conclusion, I summarize my argument and identify some areas for further thought and action.

As the "Preface to the Series" states, this series "(1) examines modern/postmodern culture from a missional point of view; (2) develops the theological agenda that the church in modern culture must address in order to recover its own integrity; and (3) tests fresh conceptualizations of the nature and mission of the church as it engages modern culture." Those are precisely the aims that this book seeks to advance through a very specific analysis of the threats to and possibilities for living faithfully in a fragmented world.

1

Living with Our History

One of the most important lessons that the church can learn from *After Virtue* is implicit in the structure and approach of the book. In that book, MacIntyre narrates the history of two ethical theories, one springing from the Enlightenment, the other from Aristotle. For MacIntyre, telling these stories constitutes an argument about morality. Note that the story is not just an illustration of an argument or an example to aid understanding. The story *is* the argument.

In later chapters, we will consider the force of MacIntyre's argument for some form of the Aristotelian tradition. What concerns us here is not which tradition MacIntyre commends or whether he is right to commend it; rather, what concerns us is the form of MacIntyre's argument. For him, the confrontation between these two traditions can be adjudicated only by attending to their histories. These traditions are not two disembodied arguments whose strengths and weaknesses can be captured in a list and then compared. The very identification of them as "traditions" means that they have a history. MacIntyre teaches us that attending to

that history—telling the stories of these traditions—
itself constitutes an argument that may or may not commend a particular tradition.

Like these traditions, the church also has a history.
Often, we study this history and tell it for seemingly triv-
ial reasons—just to "know more" or to "add to our
knowledge." So, we may memorize dates and names to
impress our friends. Sometimes we will study the history
in order to understand Christian doctrine better. For example, we give considerable attention to the early church
councils. At times, we may give much attention to peri-
ods when the church's history overlaps significantly
with other historical concerns, such as the impact of
revivalism on American culture. But with a few notable
exceptions, we have done very little to tell the history of
the church as an argument for Christian faith.[3]

History-as-Argument

There are many reasons for our neglect of history-as-
argument. Two are particularly important. First, we
have tended to think of arguments on a model that was
given to us by philosophy. On this model—there are others, but this one has predominated—arguments are con-
structed syllogistically; they are disembodied, ahistorical
arguments for disembodied, ahistorical people. People
have no history that influences their reason; positions
likewise have no history that enters into an argument.
One of MacIntyre's primary aims is to expose the failure
of this presupposition, what in ethical theory he calls
"the failure of the Enlightenment project." MacIntyre
exposes this failure not through a syllogistic argument,
but by telling the history of the Enlightenment project
so that we see its regrettable results. By narrating the

failure of this project in moral terms, MacIntyre exposes the failure of the presupposition underlying ahistorical, disembodied arguments. From MacIntyre, the church should start learning how to tell its story as an argument for its witness to the gospel.

The second reason that the church has neglected the notion of history-as-argument is a fear that our history would be an argument against rather than for the gospel. Certainly there are grounds for this fear. The church has often sinned, and sinned greatly, against God and humanity in the name of the gospel. But our fear is misplaced for several reasons. First, it mistakenly confuses the church and the gospel. The gospel is not just a message; it is the reality of God's redeeming activity through Jesus Christ.[4] The church is a human community called into existence by God and sustained by God as a witness to the gospel, but the church is not the gospel. The history of the church is the story of how far the church is from the gospel, but it is also the history of how God uses the church to witness to God's redemption of creation. When the church is unfaithful, God still makes the church a witness to the kingdom by God's judgment: "The time has come for judgment to begin with the household of God" (1 Pet. 4:17). Moreover, the history of the church's failures is the history of the church's recognition of its distance from the gospel of Jesus Christ. That is, even the failures of the church may witness to the gospel when those failures are recognized and properly confessed. Of course, we must be careful not to turn this into an argument for more sin in the church, as Paul imagines his interlocutors doing in Romans 6. Nevertheless, the point remains: The church is not the gospel, so we must become more adept at telling the story of the church and the gospel so that we witness to the gospel.

Second, our fear of our history disembodies our faith. At the same time that we avoid the church's history we also avoid the history of the gospel at work in this world. This double neglect disembodies the gospel of Jesus Christ and renders it unreal in the world. One of the reasons that there is such a gap between most formal theology and the life of the church is that formal theology disembodies the gospel. Real people and real lives have a history. We are not merely intellects processing logical arguments; we are human beings seeking a way of life. Week after week, preachers and other believers labor mightily to overcome this neglect and to embody the faith without significant help from theology. Now, there is certainly a place for formal theology. Indeed, this book is an example of what I am criticizing. My plea is that we recognize the limitations of this approach and give more attention to history-as-argument.

If we do not attend to our history, in addition to confusing the gospel and the church and disembodying the gospel, we will become victims of our past. If we do not attend to our history, then the forces that have shaped us and brought us to this point will determine our fate. They become so familiar and comfortable that they become the very air that we breathe. As a consequence, we do not recognize the betrayals of the gospel that have taken place, and we do not identify the distance between the gospel and the church. In God's love for this world, God has never allowed the church to be completely faithless. God's judgment purifies, and a remnant always remains as faithful witnesses. In these instances, the church's fear of its history results in a failure to recognize and confess our sin, and leads us into God's judgment so that we might be purified.

If we do not attend to our history, others also become victims of our past. The church has continually mistaken its judgment for God's will. History is replete with peoples who have been victimized by the church's mistaken judgments. As we continually deny these mistakes or suppress our memory of them, the church is bound to move on to other oppressive mistakes. We need continually to tell our story as confession of our unfaithfulness, so that the world may see beyond the church to the gospel and so that we may all maintain a healthy suspicion of the church's confident pronouncements of God's will. In such a way, the church will be less likely to victimize others.

Often, the church denies its history in order to protect its existence. If we admit our past and its mistakes, this seems very much like an admission that the church has no necessary claim on existence. But that reasoning is contrary to the gospel. In the gospel, the church knows that we have been *given* everything necessary to life and salvation in Jesus Christ. In Jesus Christ, God has claimed this world for redemption: the church witnesses to that redemption; it has no need to claim this world for itself. The church's only reason for existence is as a witness to the gospel of Jesus Christ. Therefore, the church is free to tell its story as confession, and in so doing is free itself to witness to the kingdom.

In addition to denying our past, another mistake we can make is glorifying our past. In other words, rather than coping with the failures of the past by denying that we have a history, we may cope with the failures of the past by glorifying our successes and ignoring our failures.[5] Instead of a blanket denial of the past, we indulge in a selective denial. This is a serious temptation in Western culture, most especially in the United States, where the church can claim considerable influence on our culture. Looking back, we can glorify the past and lament the loss of the good old days when Christians were the majority or society at least accepted Christian values. Having made this step, we may then conclude that the mission of the church is to reassert this dominance in society.

This approach is easily identifiable today in much of the political action pursued in the name of Christianity. The church in the United States, more than any other nation marked by Western culture, looks to the past as a glorious time of Christian rule to which we must return if we are to turn away God's wrath. Two arguments stand against this approach. First, it represents the error of "Constantinianism."[6] Where denying our past may be a result of confusing the kingdom and the church, glorifying our past is often the result of confusing the kingdom and society. Since the conversion of the Emperor Constantine to Christianity and the subsequent rise of Christianity as the dominant religion of the empire in the early decades of the fourth century, the church has continually fallen into the error of thinking that the mission of the church was not to make disciples of Jesus Christ among all nations, but to rule the world by exercising power through political structures. According to this way of thinking, the mission of the church in the modern world is, first, to gain control of the political processes so that the laws of the land reflect Christian values and, second, to form church members into good citizens who will sustain the political life of the nation. In this way, our glorious Christian past will be revived for today.

This Constantinian understanding of the mission of the church may be born of a very commendable conviction that the church and the kingdom are embodied, visible realities today, but it ends up mistaking a human creation—the empire, the nation—for God's kingdom. When this happens, the existence of the kingdom and the church are thought to depend upon a particular state of affairs, such as a political system, a growing economy, a particular social structure, or the rule of a particular person. If we have confused the kingdom and a particular state of affairs, when that state of affairs changes we become anxious about the existence of the kingdom and the church. We then mistakenly think that the mission of the church is to bring about, or help bring about, a return to the state of affairs upon which the kingdom depends.

Much of what passes for Christian mission today is motivated by precisely this way of thinking: the church actively promotes a return to some past state of affairs so that the kingdom may once again be present—so that God may once again "bless America." At this point, however, we have badly muddled the work of the gospel and the relationship between the church, the world, and the kingdom. Certainly, the good news of Jesus Christ reveals God's work in this world. That work is not just a hoped-for future; it is a present reality. That reality is not just an interior state of being in the believer; it is a way of living out our social relationships. But that reality is not captive to some particular culture. The gospel has been powerfully at work throughout many cultures, in all kinds of political systems and economic circumstances, and has encompassed many different rulers, nations, and languages. Nor is the reality of the gospel captive to the past. It is presently at work in powerful ways that, by the grace of the Holy Spirit, we may discern throughout our world.

The temptation to glorify our past because of a Constantinian confusion of the kingdom and society disables that discernment and leads to a betrayal of the mission of the church. In such a situation, our task is to learn from the past how to disentangle our vision of church, world, and gospel so that we can see the gospel at work today.

In addition to confusing the kingdom and society, when the church glorifies our history we also mistake the character of the kingdom. The gospel does reveal the glory of the kingdom of God in Jesus Christ, but it is the same glory that Jesus Christ revealed, the glory of servanthood: "Whoever wishes to become great among you must be your servant, and whoever wishes to be first among you must be slave of all. For the Son of Man came not to be served but to serve, and to give his life a ransom for many" (Mark 10:44–45). This kind of glory is not the glory that is sought by those who confuse the kingdom and society. Just as Jesus Christ came as a servant, so also the church fulfills its mission to witness to this gospel by serving. Those who glorify the past seek a return to the past by imposing the rule of the church on society. But the mission of the church is not to impose the gospel or some state of affairs on the world in order to bring the kingdom. Rather, the church is called to witness to the gospel. The gospel is a gift, not an imposition, and the church's faithfulness to the gospel is measured in part by its unwillingness to impose its rule upon society.

Of course, to some this may sound like a recommendation for a weak church that can be manipulated by society. In fact, however, the opposite is the case. As I will later argue in detail in Chapters 4 and 5, for the church to live and witness faithfully in our world, the church must be a highly disciplined, courageous community. It is the church that willingly adopts the power of the world that does not need discipline or courage—until it is brought face-to-face with God's judgment.

Finally, we must note that when the church succumbs to the temptation to glorify the past, it usually does so by narrowing its view of the kingdom to one particular state of affairs. When this happens, the work of the gospel becomes restricted—often to one class, one race, sometimes even one sex, at least as the primary participants in the gospel. That is, the glorification of the past usually identifies one particular tradition, time, or place as *the* moment of faithfulness. This has the effect of excluding other people, times, and places from the possibility of faithfulness. This narrowing of the kingdom, then, betrays the commission to make disciples of *all the peoples*.

The Church's History in Western Culture

MacIntyre teaches us that living faithfully in this world means that the church must live with its history, neither denying that history nor glorifying it. For the purposes of this book, the history that will concern us is the history of the church in Western culture, that is, in European civilizations, particularly since the Enlightenment.[7] Indeed, "living with our history" means that the church must live with the effects of its influence on our culture. After Constantine—that is, after Christianity became

the favored religion of the empire—the church became
the most powerful force in Western society. Political
structures, educational institutions, social forms, and
the theories that sustained them can all be traced to the
influence of the church. That these institutions, forms,
and theories took different and often conflicting shape
does not change the fact that the power and language of
the church was claimed by all of them. When rebellion
and revolution were preached, they too came to us
determined by the forms and languages of the church.

In European civilization, intellectual, political, and
cultural history and practices can be understood only
in relation to the history of the church. Given this, the
history of the church becomes a terribly tangled web
and a fearful burden. The church can be implicated in
the worst events of our past: the Medieval church and
the Crusades, the German Church Movement and
National Socialism, the American church and slavery,
the Dutch Reformed Church and apartheid, and the
list could go on. No matter how controversial and complex the church's involvement is or how powerfully
some in the church resisted these movements, it is still
true that the church has been a dominant force in
Western culture.

The dominance of the church in the history of our
culture becomes particularly problematic as we move
into a time when that dominance is only a memory.
Although we live in a culture that has been largely
shaped by the influence of the church and by reactions
to the church, other forces now dominate our culture.
In the following two chapters we will look more closely
at this situation. For now, I want to explore some ways
in which this situation provides some unique threats

and opportunities for the church to live faithfully and witness to the gospel of Jesus Christ.

As the church increasingly recognizes its minority status in Western culture, one obvious response will be to attempt to regain dominance in our culture. Tied into this strategy is the Constantinian presumption criticized above. It is in error both theologically and historically.[8] The better response is to ask ourselves: "What must the church do in order to live and witness faithfully as a minority in a culture where we were once the majority?" This is the question that brings into focus the history of the church in Western culture and how we today are to live with our history.

There are two sources of instruction that are of limited help to us. They are helpful because they point us to other times and places when the church has been in a minority situation. They are limited because in neither instance did the minority church have to come to terms with a history of dominance. One source of guidance is the early church. Certainly, for the first three hundred years of its life, the church was a persecuted minority. Although sometimes admired, Christians had little or no social and political status *as Christians.* As Christians, they were also vulnerable legally and economically. Some who became Christians had already achieved some social, economic, and political power, but by becoming Christians they risked losing what they had gained. So, in the early history of the church, the church existed as a minority in a larger culture that was frequently hostile. Moreover, the early church witnessed to the gospel in the midst of many competing claims to truth. The Mediterranean world of the early centuries was filled with a plethora of religions and gods to believe in.

These two characteristics of the early church—its minority status and the diversity of beliefs in the culture around it—reflect the conditions faced by the church in Western culture today. We may learn from the early church some lessons for how to live faithfully today, but we will also discover some limits to what we can learn from them. John Howard Yoder points out a number of lessons to learn from the early church about sustaining belief in the Lordship of Jesus Christ even though his followers are not mighty or numerous by the world's standards; about using language from the culture to communicate the gospel of Jesus Christ; about how to witness to those in power; and other lessons (Yoder 1984:chap. 1). But what Yoder does not identify so clearly are the effects on the church today of the church's past impact on our culture. The early church did not have to live with the history of its having shaped the Mediterranean culture. So, for example, where the early church knew that it was encountering an alien, resistant, even hostile culture, the contemporary church in the West tends to think of the culture as benign, if not friendly, toward the gospel. Where the early church knew that its message was new and strange, the contemporary church presents its message as familiar and comfortable. Where the early church sought to make its message understood, the contemporary church assumes that it is understood and seeks to persuade its hearers to accept what they understand. In each of these instances, and many others, we have something to learn from the early church.

The contemporary church, however, faces some challenges not faced by the early church, because, as already noted, the early church did not have a history with which it had to live. For example, the early church did not have to answer for the way that its life had been intertwined with injustice, such as the church's support for slavery and segregation in the American South and apartheid in South Africa. Nor did the early church have a legacy of anti-Semitism to confess. Nor did the early church have a history of visible support for unjust and immoral rulers. All of this history has an effect on how we are to live faithfully today, and the practices of the early church give us limited guidance here.

Moreover, as we will see in the next chapter, the contemporary church encounters many apparently "Christian" words, concepts, and practices in our culture that are left over from the church's impact on that culture. These words, concepts, and practices may seem to convey the gospel, but in the end they betray the gospel because they have lost their rootage in the gospel. The early church did not face this danger because they knew that the culture they were encountering was not Christian. We can learn from the early church what it means to take language captive for the gospel, but we face a special danger because of the lingering effects of the church on our culture.

In addition to the early church, we may also find some limited guidance from the experience of Western missionaries and churches in countries outside European civilization. Of course, because of missionary activity and the expansion of Western political and economic power aided by technology, European civilization has had a global impact. For these reasons the Western church has much to learn from churches in these other countries.[9] Third World churches are producing a number of theologians and church leaders who are addressing the Western church with challenging questions. These observers often see us more clearly than we see ourselves. They challenge our complicity with Western political and economic powers, and they expose our cultural blindness.

Likewise, missiologists and other Westerners who have been shaped by non-Western churches have some profound lessons to teach us. Two of those missiologists are William Dyrness and Lesslie Newbigin. In *How Does America Hear the Gospel?*, Dyrness (1989), who taught in the Philippines for many years, teaches us what many other missionaries have been saying, that we in the West need to look at our culture from a missionary perspective. For many decades we have been critically attentive to other cultures as we have sought to present the gospel, but we have not been critically attentive to our own culture. It has been as natural to us as the air we breathe, and, as a result, we have not thought of our own culture as a threat to our faithfulness or as an object of careful analysis. Now, through the kind of work that Dyrness represents, we are learning to approach our own culture as missionaries. Newbigin, who served several decades in South India, including nearly twenty years as a bishop of the Church of South India, "retired" to England in 1974. In retirement, he has turned his attention to the spiritual plight of the West. He has written a series of books (Newbigin 1986, 1989, 1991) that analyze Western culture from a missionary perspective. As a Westerner who has spent much of his life ministering in India, Newbigin offers some powerful analyses and insights. He is particularly sensitive to the effects of the Enlightenment on Western culture and to the challenge that represents for communicating the gospel.

Although Dyrness and Newbigin bring missionary insights from the Third World that we will draw on in the following chapters, they do not attend to the life of the church in the history of Western culture as closely as we will. They concentrate instead on the interaction of the gospel and culture, rather than the church and culture. As a result, neither one develops a full and clear account of the church's relationship to Western culture or of the changing status of the church and its significance for the mission of the church.

The First Lesson

How are we to live faithfully as the church in our culture? The first lesson that MacIntyre teaches us is that in order to live faithfully, the church must learn to live with its history. Learning to live with our history means learning to distinguish among the church, the kingdom, and the world as we tell our story. If we learn to make these distinctions, then we will neither deny nor glorify the history of the church. Instead, we will be able to bear witness to the gospel in the midst of the church's faithfulness and unfaithfulness. By attending to our history, we will also learn to think like missionaries about our own culture. If we learn to think about our own history and culture in this way, then we will be able to discern the threats to and possibilities for living faithfully in the midst of our fragmented world.

2

Fragmented Worlds

MacIntyre begins *After Virtue* with "a disquieting suggestion" that we live in a fragmented world.[10] He draws out the implications of this suggestion through the following scenario:

Imagine that the natural sciences were to suffer the effects of a catastrophe. A series of environmental disasters are blamed by the general public on the scientists. Widespread riots occur, laboratories are burnt down, physicists are lynched, books and instruments are destroyed. Finally, a Know-Nothing political movement takes power and successfully abolishes science teaching in schools and universities, imprisoning and executing the remaining scientists. Later still there is a reaction against this destructive movement and enlightened people seek to revive science, although they have largely forgotten what it was. But all they possess are fragments; a knowledge of experiments detached from any knowledge of the theoretical context which gave them significance;

parts of theories unrelated either to the other bits and pieces of theory which they possess or to experiment; instruments whose use has been forgotten; half-chapters from books, single pages from articles, not always fully legible because torn and charred. None the less all these fragments are reembodied in a set of practices which go under the revived names of physics, chemistry, and biology. Adults argue with each other about the respective merits of relativity theory, evolutionary theory, and phlogiston theory, although they possess only a very partial knowledge of each. Children learn by heart the surviving portions of the periodic table and recite as incantations some of the theorems of Euclid. Nobody, or almost nobody, realises that what they are doing is not natural science in any proper sense at all. For everything that they do and say conforms to certain canons of consistency and coherence and those contexts which would be needed to understand what they are doing have been lost, perhaps irretrievably (MacIntyre 1984:1).

Building on this imaginary scenario, MacIntyre argues that

in the actual world which we inhabit the language of morality is in the same state of grave disorder as the language of natural science in the world which I described. What we possess, if this view is true, are the fragments of a conceptual scheme, parts of which now lack those contexts from which their significance derived. We possess indeed simulacra of morality, we continue to use

many of the key expressions. But we have—very
largely, if not entirely—lost our comprehension,
both theoretical and practical, of morality (:2).

The importance of this claim and MacIntyre's support-
ing arguments cannot be overstated, even though we
might want to make some adjustments (Horton and
Mendus 1994; Milbank 1990; below, Chapter 4). His
narrative displays the ways in which our culture lost
the conceptual scheme(s) that gave meaning to our
morality and thus ended up with only fragments. My
intention in this chapter is to describe that fragmentation, show how the church participates in it and, consequently, often mistakes our disordered language for
well-ordered language and has only a simulacra of
Christian mission.

Pluralism Is Not the Problem

Before we can understand the significance of the fragmentation of our culture, we must examine a pervasive
description of contemporary culture that seems very
much like this concept of fragmentation, but which ultimately misleads us about the changes and challenges
that the church faces today. One of the most popular
ways of characterizing the challenge of the modern
world to Christian mission is to say that we live in a
pluralistic world. This pluralism is supposed to be a
particular challenge for a church that has lived in a
monolithic world for so long and has not had to com-
pete with other claims to truth. On the basis of this
characterization, many have looked to the early church
and to missionary situations in the Third World for
guidance, as we saw in the previous chapter.

The second lesson that we learn from MacIntyre's *After Virtue* is that we live, not in a pluralistic world, but among fragmented worlds. As we will see, this characterization makes the challenge of our situation much deeper than pluralism. After we examine the more familiar description of pluralism and its limitations for describing our situation, we will consider how to meet the challenges of living faithfully among fragmented worlds.

Pluralism, as I am using it here, describes a world of competing outlooks, traditions, or claims to truth. It pictures a culture made up of coherent, integral communities, traditions, or positions that can be clearly differentiated from one another. Although they disagree and may often be in conflict, where these disagreements are located and why they arise are generally clear to everyone. One's identity—as an individual or community—is clear, the convictions that constitute that identity are coherent, and the life that follows from those convictions is determined. When one of these communities breaks down, we can say how it has failed. So even though there are many competing communities, identities, or positions, pluralism describes a situation in which these competing outlooks are coherent and clearly defined.

MacIntyre argues that characterizing our culture in terms of pluralism is misleading and obscures the real challenge that we face. In his analysis, Western culture is fragmented, not pluralistic. It is incoherent; our lives are lived piecemeal, not whole. The disagreements that we have are difficult to resolve because we cannot locate them within some coherent position or community. We do not live in a world filled with competing outlooks; we live in a world that has fallen apart.[11]

Although pluralism is often used to describe the new situation and challenges facing the church, it more nearly describes the world in which I grew up in the American Midwest and South in the 1950s and 1960s. We are used to thinking of American culture in the 1950s and early 1960s as monolithic. However, in those years, we were all acutely aware that we lived in a world of competing communities and traditions. The melting pot was full of unmeltable goods.

In order to make this claim clearer, let's consider the competition between two groups of Baptists. I grew up as the son of a pastor in the National Association of Free Will Baptists. Free Will Baptists number about 250,000 and are located primarily in the South and Midwest. Their theology is Arminian (it is possible to believe in Christ, then fall away from him). At the time I was growing up, Free Will Baptists were also separatist fundamentalists (many so-called Christians really are not Christians, and we should keep separate from them). We were very clear about the differences between us and other churches, even other Baptists. If we were told that someone was a Free Will Baptist, we could say clearly how that person would be different from a Southern Baptist. Southern Baptists believed that once you were saved, you could not lose your salvation, so they were not nearly so careful about Christian living as were Free Will Baptists. We were sure Southern Baptists really were "Christians who don't drink in front of each other." Southern Baptist women did not dress as modestly as Free Will Baptists (they used more makeup, wore more jewelry, and some wore trousers), and Southern Baptist men were not as trustworthy in business as Free Will Baptists.

As with these two close relatives, so also with other communities and traditions: if we knew which church a person belonged to, we could tell you about his or her life. Nazarenes, the Christian Church, the Presbyterians, the Methodists, the Catholics, and in larger cities, Jews, were part of our world. But it was a pluralistic world populated by coherent communities with clear boundaries.

Certainly, pluralism may be used to describe any number of situations. The most helpful use of the term identifies the kind of situation I have been describing, where competing communities and traditions are relatively coherent, clearly distinguishable entities. Today, we are often drawn to use the term because we live in a world where more options are present and where the differences among the options are greater than they used to be. It is true that there are more options today: I did not grow up in a world where Hindus, Buddhists, and Muslims were my neighbors. So both the variety and differences are greater today. But to think that pluralism captures the real significance of the changes in our culture misconstrues the change and the challenge that it represents.

Living Among Fragments

In order to live faithfully today, we must recognize that we have not moved from a monolithic world into a pluralistic world; rather, we have moved from a time when our communities were relatively coherent and clear to a time when our communities and traditions have become fragmented. Certainly, some coherent communities still exist, but these are communities that for various reasons have not been a part of our cultural change. For example, the Amish, as well as Hasidic Jews, remain

relatively coherent as communities because they have
not participated in the larger culture. Recent Muslim
immigrants have coherent communities because their
participation in Western culture is relatively recent.[12] In
contrast, communities like Free Will Baptists and
Southern Baptists have fragmented so much that one
can no longer be sure of properly identifying or describing a member of either tradition. (Of course, Free Will
Baptists would want to say that you can still tell them
from Presbyterians.)

The church in the West is fragmented because its life
has for so long been intertwined with the larger culture.
As that culture has fragmented, so also has the church.
MacIntyre's narrative of this fragmentation centers on
morality. He shows that moral schemes that were previ-
ously coherent depended for their coherence upon a
conceptual scheme that gave a description of (1)
"where" humans are on a moral landscape, (2) where
they should be, and (3) how to get from where they are
to where they should be. In a lengthy and powerful
analysis, MacIntyre shows how and why modern culture
abandoned the second element of this scheme—any
convictions about where humans should be—our *telos*
(goal, purpose, end). Once any notion of *telos* is abandoned, we are left with where humans are and what we
should do, but what we should do—morality—makes no
sense apart from a *telos*. Therefore our moral language,
practice, and concepts linger as fragments of a previ-
ously coherent account. As time goes on, these moral
fragments appear arbitrary—mere exercises of power or
expressions of emotion.

This same fragmentation has deeply affected the
moral life of the church, but its effects are not limited to

morality. The entire life of the church has been deeply affected by this fragmentation. If we cling to pluralism and neglect fragmentation as a description of our situation, we will become more vulnerable over time and will cease to live and witness faithfully. We will have the appearance of life and health, but it will be only simulacra of the church's calling.

We can guard against this happening by attending to two areas of the church's life that are radically challenged by this fragmentation. Our analysis will not be exhaustive; rather, it will be suggestive of the kinds of threats the church faces and possible ways of living faithfully. As we look at these areas of fragmentation in the life of the church, we will observe a number of interwoven complications. We will discover that when we lose the *telos* or overarching conceptual scheme that gives meaning to language and practice, then that language and practice becomes more easily assimilated to other purposes and other sources of meaning. We will also discover that fragmentation affects both the internal and external life of the church. That is, because the life of the church has been so intertwined with the culture, the fragmentation of church and culture means that there are fragments of the church's influence present in the larger culture. The church may easily mistake these fragments as coherent understandings of the gospel, and, as a result, fall into serious miscommunication that is almost impossible to recognize and untangle. Finally, as we explore this fragmentation, we will discover that individuals live fragmented lives. One moment their language and practice is ordered to one community and tradition; the next moment, another community and tradition determines their language and

practice. Once again, this kind of incoherence is very
difficult to identify and untangle, but with MacIntyre's
help we may begin to discern some of this incoherence.

One area of the life of the church that is deeply
affected by fragmentation is our worship. As the
Westminster Catechism states, "the chief end of
[humanity] is to glorify God and enjoy [God] forever."
When this *telos* is lost and (pseudo)worship continues,
then our practice of worship may appear healthy but be
ordered by the wrong end. Such a situation is not new;
Isaiah describes just such circumstances:

> Hear the word of the LORD,
>   you rulers of Sodom!
> Listen to the teaching of our God,
>   you people of Gomorrah!
> What to me is the multitude of your sacrifices?
>   says the LORD;
> I have had enough of burnt offerings of rams
>   and the fat of fed beasts;
> I do not delight in the blood of bulls,
>   or of lambs, or of goats.
>
> When you come to appear before me,
>   who asked this from your hand?
> Trample my courts no more;
>   bringing offerings is futile;
>   incense is an abomination to me.
> New moon and sabbath and calling of convocation—
>   I cannot endure solemn assemblies with iniquity.
> Your new moons and your appointed festivals
>   my soul hates;
> they have become a burden to me,
>   I am weary of bearing them.

When you stretch out your hands,
    I will hide my eyes from you;
even though you make many prayers,
    I will not listen;
    your hands are full of blood.
Wash yourselves; make yourselves clean;
    remove the evil of your doings
    from before my eyes;
cease to do evil;
    learn to do good;
seek justice,
    rescue the oppressed,
defend the orphan,
    plead for the widow. (Isa. 1:10–17)

Here, Isaiah describes a community that clearly engages enthusiastically in worship. They bring their best animals as sacrifices, and they have even added new times of worship. But in spite of this care and enthusiasm, the community is under the threat of God's judgment because they have forgotten the purpose of worship. Their lives are so fragmented that they can "worship" the God of justice, the God of the oppressed, but not live out that conviction in the rest of their lives. Apparently, outside of formal worship, their lives are ordered by other ends: prosperity, security, pleasure.

Like these ancient Israelites, the people of God in the Western church have forgotten that the purpose of worship is to teach us to glorify God and enjoy God forever in the whole of our lives. Because our practice of worship has been severed from this end, and because our own lives are governed by competing, incompatible ends, our worship becomes disordered, even when it

appears orderly and enthusiastic. As a result of this disordering, we try to make worship serve other purposes.
So, for example, if we accept another version of the
human *telos*—that we are to be happy, well-adjusted
people—then we expect worship to be a kind of mass
therapy session that makes us "feel better." Or if we
believe that the human *telos* is to be successful profes-
sionally, then we expect worship to be a kind of mass
pep rally that energizes us for the week ahead. We can
even distort the purpose of worship by believing that the
human *telos* is a happy, healthy family. And so we
expect that worship will be ordered to that end.

The difficulty here, of course, is that all of these seem
like such admirable, faithful purposes: who wants to be
maladjusted, unsuccessful, and unhappy? The mistake
that we make is that these purposes disorder our worship;
that is, they are proper consequences of worship rightly
ordered to the purpose of glorifying God and enjoying God
forever. Take, for instance, the quest for a happy, well-
adjusted life. In connection with this quest, its defenders
ask, "Should not worship make us feel better? We all have
difficult, demanding lives. Shouldn't worship be a place of
healing and encouragement?" Of course, worship should
make us feel better and encourage us, but it properly does
so when it is ordered to the right end. If we approach worship as a mass therapy session, then the effect of worship
is to make us feel better and encourage us by changing our
emotional state and our self-perception. However, the
proper end of worship is to reorient our lives and give us a
vision of God's reality. If our worship is ordered by this
end, then we will not merely feel better, we will be blessed,
and our perception of the world, not just our perception of
ourselves, will be changed.

Worship will indeed make us feel better and encourage us; but when properly ordered, worship places these results within a coherent community and tradition, not a fragmented, incoherent life. Properly ordered worship will engage the whole of our lives. That is, properly ordered worship integrates all of life into a coherent whole so that what we confess and enact in communal worship extends over the rest of our lives. Because our culture and our lives are so fragmented, this demand for coherence appears strange and entails pain and struggle. But to live faithfully in a fragmented world requires just this kind of ordering in our worship.[13]

Because this fragmentation and disordering of our worship is so subtle, one additional insight from MacIntyre may help us discern and correct our disorder. In MacIntyre's discussion of "practices," he distinguishes between "internal" and "external" goods (MacIntyre 1984:187–191).[14] External goods are precisely that—goods that may be acquired through some activity but that are themselves external to that activity. On the other hand, internal goods are goods intrinsic to an activity; they cannot be truly conceived, experienced, or understood apart from a particular kind of activity. So, for example, someone may play basketball to achieve external goods, such as status, fame, a college scholarship, or a multimillion-dollar professional contract. Although these goods are acquired through playing basketball, they really exist independently of basketball. Or one could play basketball in order to achieve goods internal to the game—participating in a team endeavor, the pleasure of physical exercise, the thrill of bodily movement ordered toward excellence. These goods cannot be conceived, experienced, or understood apart from the actual *practice* of playing basketball or some similar sport. To play basketball for internal goods makes basketball a practice.

This distinction between external and internal goods can help us discern the disorder of our worship when we ask ourselves to which of these our worship is ordered. Do we seek through our worship goods that are extrinsic to worship? Or do we seek goods intrinsic to worship, goods that cannot be conceived, experienced, or understood apart from worship? To achieve humanity's true end—to glorify and enjoy God—simply *is* to worship; one cannot conceive a way of glorifying and enjoying God apart from the practice of worship. So, if the things that we are seeking in and through worship can be conceived apart from worship, our worship is disordered. More strongly still, in biblical terms worship that is ordered toward some end other than glorifying and enjoying God is idolatry. In our fragmented world and lives, we need to attend carefully to our "order" of worship in order to live faithfully.

Another area of contemporary fragmentation that has a tremendous impact on the possibility of living faithfully is the continued presence in our culture of leftover Christian language and symbols. In our culture the cross has become a fragmented symbol, as the following story reveals.[15] Recently, a friend went into a jewelry store in the town where I live, Santa Barbara, California. When the clerk asked if she could help him, he said, "Yes, I would like to look at some crosses." She replied, "Would you like to see ones with the little man on them, or ones without?"

For many years in our culture the cross has been worn by people with no commitment to Jesus Christ and even by those who clearly despise the way of Jesus. But even in those situations the cross was a coherent symbol; people could say what it stood for, even if it had no personal significance for them. In the clerk's reply, we have a perfect example of a fragmented symbol; for her, as for many others, there is no community and no larger conceptual scheme to give the cross meaning.

The fact that the cross, and not, for instance, a hammer and sickle, is the symbol in question indicates the confluence of the church's history in our culture and the present fragmentation of our culture. This fragmented symbol is a powerful warning of the difficulties faced by the church in its attempts to live faithfully. Because Christianity has such a long history of influence in Western culture, many of the words, symbols, concepts, and activities of our culture appear to have their origins and meaning bound up in the church's witness to Jesus Christ. However, because we live in fragmented worlds today, those words, symbols, concepts, and activities may be profoundly deceptive. Take, for example, the simple declaration of the good news, "Jesus Christ died on the cross for the forgiveness of sins." The words "Jesus Christ" are very common, more common perhaps outside the church than inside, where they are simply words of profanity. As we have already seen, although the cross is pervasive in our culture, it is a fragmented symbol, or worse, a symbol of racist and sexist oppression. As L. Gregory Jones has recently shown, the notion of forgiveness is a deeply fragmented concept and practice in our culture; it has been captured by the therapeutic and eclipsed by violence (Jones 1995). Cornelius Plantinga (1995) has done the same for our understanding of sin.

Without saying so explicitly or at length, these analyses point up some of the deeply fragmented areas of our lives and culture. For the church to live faithfully, we must recognize the dynamic of this fragmentation. As Isaiah's oracle and MacIntyre's parable point out, a fragmented world may be marked by the appearance of a lively faithfulness in language and practice. The church may appear to be using all the right words and engaging in all the right activities, but if the church and the culture are fragmented, then that appearance is profoundly deceptive.

The Second Lesson

MacIntyre's second lesson for the church is that we live among fragments. In the midst of this fragmentation, we may appear to be doing many "Christian" things; but if our activity is not ordered to our proper end, then that activity is unfaithful. This unfaithfulness is greatly complicated by the very nature of our situation that makes it difficult for us to discern our unfaithfulness. In order to untangle these complications a bit further, we turn next, with MacIntyre's help, to the history that has led to our fragmentation.

3

The Failure of the Enlightenment Project

As we saw in the previous chapter, we live today among fragmented worlds. The first half of *After Virtue* identifies the source of this fragmentation by narrating "the failure of the Enlightenment project." This project seeks a rational justification for morality that is independent of any particular convictions, especially theological convictions. At one level, it may be understood as an attempt to end the conflicts in Europe that were rooted in religious differences. At another level, this project may be read as the rejection of the classical moral tradition. MacIntyre shows that today this project and its failure lies at the root of the problems that both occupy academic philosophers *and* afflict our everyday social life (MacIntyre 1984:chap. 4).

The Culture's Enlightenment Project

After narrating the history of successive attempts to achieve an independent rational justification for morality in the work of Hume (who sought justification in the passions), Diderot (desire), Kant (reason), and Kierkegaard (choice), MacIntyre argues that these attempts failed, not because they looked to the wrong sources for justifying morality, but because they had in common a particular way of characterizing the problem; in short, they were all seeking to achieve "the Enlightenment project." This project was bound to fail, MacIntyre argues, because it misconstrued the moral tradition that it had inherited.

According to MacIntyre, the moral tradition previous to the Enlightenment depended upon a threefold structure: (1) humanity as we are; (2) humanity as we should be; (3) how we can get from where we are to where we should be (MacIntyre 1984:54). The Enlightenment project abandoned any notion of "humanity as we should be," because any account of who we should be depends upon a view of the true end of humanity that is rooted in particular convictions—the very thing that the Enlightenment sought to avoid. So the Enlightenment project abandoned this threefold structure and attempted to justify morality apart from any particular view of what humanity could be if we realized our true end. As a result, the Enlightenment left us with humanity as we are and moral instruction for how to get from where we are to…? Because the Enlightenment abandoned all accounts of where we should be, it could give no description of the purpose of morality. Thus moral precepts lacked the structure that had given them meaning and coherence. Consequently, MacIntyre argues, "the Enlightenment project had to fail" (MacIntyre 1984:chap. 5). We still have some of the language and practices of morality, but they exist only in fragments, apart from the overall structure that gave them meaning. This fragmented morality appears to have no justification, for it has been deprived of the very convictions that give it meaning. Increasingly, then, morality seems to be merely a set of (often personal) preferences.

As a result of this history, our culture is largely shaped by emotivism—"the doctrine that all evaluative judgments and more specifically all moral judgments are *nothing but* expressions of preference, expressions of attitude or feeling, insofar as they are moral or evaluative in character" (MacIntyre 1984:11–12). In such a culture

> moral judgments, being expressions of attitude or feeling, are neither true nor false; and disagreement in moral judgment is not to be secured by any rational method, for there are none. It is to be secured, if at all, by producing certain non-rational effects on the emotions or attitudes of those who disagree with mine. We use moral judgments not only to express our own attitudes and feelings, but also precisely to produce such effects in others (:12).

If the church is to live faithfully in the context of an emotivist culture marked by the failure of the Enlightenment project, then we must learn a number of things from MacIntyre's account.

The Church's Enlightenment Project

In order to understand the impact of the Enlightenment project on the life of the church, we must first attend to ways in which the church is implicated in the Enlightenment project to achieve an independent rational justification for morality. Certainly, the moral tradition of the Western church, because of our involvement with our culture, has been deeply affected by the failure of the Enlightenment project. This was the concern of

the previous chapter, where we saw how the fragmentation of morality poses a serious threat to faithful living.

Of equal significance as a threat to the life of the
church is the fact that the church has carried on its
own version of the Enlightenment project in relation,
not to morality, but to the gospel. That is, just as
Western culture, in the Enlightenment project, sought
an independent rational justification for morality, so
also the Western church has sought independent rational justification for the gospel. And just as the
Enlightenment project to justify morality was bound to
fail, for the same reasons the church's version of the
Enlightenment project also had to fail.

The church's quest for an independent rational justification of the gospel has taken a number of forms. It is
clearly evident in our apologetics, where there has been
considerable debate. It is also the main theme of Hans
Frei's influential analyses of hermeneutics and modern
theology (Frei 1968, 1992, 1993). Of greatest interest
for us is the way that the church's Enlightenment project has marked our evangelism.

In contrast to the studies of apologetics, rationality,
and hermeneutics, the church's language about and
practice of evangelism has received little analysis along
these lines. In order to initiate some examination of this
tendency in evangelism, rather than examine specific
practices and programs of evangelism, I will here sketch
some general characteristics of the church's Enlightenment
project on evangelism.

The overarching characteristic of this project is the
church's attempt to commend the gospel on grounds
that have nothing to do with the gospel itself. In this
way, the church avoids any convictions particular to the

gospel or the church as the basis for justifying or commending the gospel. Two things result from this attempt. First, as with MacIntyre's narrative of the Enlightenment project on morality, the church seeks various grounds for the gospel. Commensurate with the attempts of Hume, Diderot, Kant, and Kierkegaard on behalf of morality, the church has had its thinkers who have sought to ground the gospel in accounts of the passions, desires, reason, and choice. This has been true of both academic and popular theology. For example, Kant's attempt to ground morality in reason is accompanied by an attempt to ground religion "within the bounds of reason alone." Here an account of reason that is independent of the gospel becomes the putative ground—and boundary— for religion. Likewise, Friedrich Schleiermacher's *On Religion: Speeches to Its Cultured Despisers* may be read as an evangelistic presentation of the gospel that seeks to commend the gospel on the basis of the feeling of absolute dependence. Because Schleiermacher's account of the feeling of absolute dependence is developed without reference to the gospel and does not depend upon the gospel for its meaning, his account is an expression of the church's Enlightenment project.[16]

On a more popular level, we may often hear evangelistic presentations that commend the gospel to its hearers on their terms, rather than seeking to present a coherent account of the gospel's own faithfulness. For example, Robert Schuller's widely known attempt at a "new reformation" based on self-esteem fails, not because self-esteem is the wrong way to translate the gospel for contemporary people, but because Schuller's account develops the notion of self-esteem separate from the structure of the gospel, then makes our quest for self-esteem the ground for commending the gospel (Schuller 1985). In other words, the fundamental problem with Schuller's appeal is not the notion of self-esteem itself, but the structure to which Schuller appeals for the meaning of self-esteem. Of course, if his account of self-esteem were developed within the overall structure of the gospel, then it would change significantly.

Admittedly, this is a difficult point to communicate and to grasp. As MacIntyre reminds us in his much fuller account of our moral situation, if he is right, then "we are in a condition which almost nobody recognises and which perhaps nobody at all can recognise fully" (MacIntyre 1984:4).[17] In the same way, if the church has engaged in its own Enlightenment project, then we are in a situation that few recognize and that none recognizes fully.

One way for us to begin to recognize our situation is by continuing to learn from MacIntyre's account. MacIntyre argues that the Enlightenment project on morality had to fail because it rejected any notion of humanity as we could be if we realized our *telos,* and thus it abandoned the very element that gave coherence, meaning, and persuasiveness to our moral precepts. What if the same thing has happened to the gospel in the church's own Enlightenment project? The church, when it is faithful to the gospel, gives an account of the present human situation, of humanity as God intends us to be, and of the gospel of salvation by grace as the means by which humanity moves (or, more properly, is moved) from where we are to where God intends us to be. When the church abandons the teleological conviction of where God intends humanity to be, then we are left with the project of seeking a ground for the claims of the gospel apart from the gospel itself. As MacIntyre has shown us, such a project is bound to fail.

Before we move on to consider the consequences of this failure, we should consider an objection, often directed toward MacIntyre, that may be brought against my account. To some, MacIntyre's account, and by extension my account, may appear to give no means for judging among competing convictions and traditions. In other words, our accounts appear fideistic or relativistic. However, as MacIntyre shows in a later work (MacIntyre 1988), his position does allow for rational comparison. Moreover, James Wm. McClendon, Jr., and James M. Smith have given an extensive account of evaluating and justifying religious convictions that is compatible with the position I am advocating (McClendon and Smith 1994). What our accounts preclude is the notion that there are grounds for justifying the gospel apart from the gospel itself.

To go beyond MacIntyre's account, the way for the church to justify the claims of the gospel is by living the way of life to which the gospel calls us. This way of life, as it displays the full claims of the gospel, may then be compared to other ways of life. This comparison occurs, not from some Archimedean point outside every tradition, but from within one's present tradition as one considers the competing claims.[18] In this understanding, the church commends the gospel by living according to the gospel, not by appealing to some ground outside the gospel. For this very reason then, this work is about *living faithfully* in a fragmented world: living faithfully simply *is* the Christian mission in the modern world.

So, one part of the lesson that we learn from MacIntyre's narrative of the failure of the Enlightenment project is that the church has carried on its own version of this project. We will be able to live faithfully in a fragmented world only as we develop our ability to discern how and where we have engaged in this Enlightenment project that is bound to fail.

Consequences of the Failure of the Enlightenment Project

We may learn something else from MacIntyre's narrative of the failure of the Enlightenment project by attending to one of the consequences of this failure. According to MacIntyre, as a result of this failure we live in a culture that is marked by three particular "characters." By characters MacIntyre means social roles that represent the moral nature of a culture. In these characters, role and personality are fused, and possibilities for action are limited by the culture. These characters provide the members of a culture "with a cultural and moral ideal" that "morally legitimates a mode of social existence" (MacIntyre 1984:29). As examples, MacIntyre points to the "Public School Headmaster, Explorer and the Engineer" for Victorian England, and the "Prussian Officer, the Professor and the Social Democrat" for Wilhelmine Germany (MacIntyre 1984:28).

In the emotivist culture that results from the failure of the Enlightenment project, our stock of characters includes the Rich Aesthete, the Therapist, and the Manager.[19] If we consider how these characters mark not only Western culture but also in very particular ways the Western church, we may gain further insight into how the church can live faithfully in a fragmented world.

In MacIntyre's account, the Rich Aesthete, who has a surplus of financial and social resources, seeks to alleviate boredom by manipulating others for the pleasure and good of the Aesthete. MacIntyre rightly warns that not all rich nor all aesthetes live out this character. Nevertheless, our culture is stocked by this "ideal." Even those who do not have the resources to live out this character may aspire to the role: living morally fragmented lives and lacking any clear *telos* for our lives, we may be captured by this character.

In the church, this character of the Rich Aesthete plays itself out in at least two ways. First, in our quest for "converts" we may be motivated more by the manipulation of others to achieve our own ends than by obedience to Christ or the desire to see others find their true *telos* in following Christ. We are especially susceptible to this when our own lives are not oriented toward loving God in obedience. Jesus warns us against this very dynamic in a slightly different setting in Matthew 6:1: "Beware of practicing your piety before others in order to be seen by them; for then you have no reward from your Father in heaven." In our culture, apparently faithful witness may be corrupted by our playing out the role of a religious Rich Aesthete when we seek converts to "add notches" or increase our status before others. Lacking an appropriate *telos,* we manipulate others through the excess of our rhetorical and emotional resources in order to increase our pleasure, alleviate our boredom, and serve our own ends.

We may play out the role of Rich Aesthete in the church in a second way, by seeking our own pleasure in worship. It is certainly right for the church to pursue beauty and excellence in worship, but that pursuit must be oriented first toward glorifying and enjoying God. When we orient worship toward giving ourselves pleasure, either through "high" liturgical worship or through "low" informal worship, we are playing out the role of the Rich Aesthete. Many analyses of what is wrong with our worship fasten on a comparison of high and low worship and argue for the superiority of one over the other. Such analyses usually miss the deeper issue of our cultural context and the subtle temptation to adopt the character of the Rich Aesthete that fulfills a (mistaken) moral ideal and legitimates a larger social mode of existence.

The second character that MacIntyre identifies in our culture is the Therapist.[20] This character has received a great deal of critical attention. In L. Gregory Jones's recent book *Embodying Forgiveness*, he devotes a chapter to how the character of the Therapist (with the collusion of the Manager, a third character we will consider below) has corrupted our practices of forgiveness (Jones 1995:chap. 2). In the previous chapter, I showed how our worship may be wrongly directed toward therapeutic ends. In this chapter, I want to consider briefly the larger problem with the character of the Therapist. As Jones, following MacIntyre, shows, the Therapist plays out our culture's acceptance and reinforcement of "the individualist realm of private feelings and values" (Jones 1995:40). That is, as the character of the Therapist is acted out in a morally fragmented culture, the Therapist enables us to adjust our private feelings and values in order to come to terms with that fragmentation. Focusing on technique and lacking any means to question our ends, the Therapist underwrites our moral fragmentation and undermines the possibility of Christian community. Thus the problem with the Therapist, as acted out in our culture, is not that God wants followers of Jesus to be unhealthy and unhappy; rather, the problem is that the Therapist locates health and happiness in the realm of private feelings and values, not in our discovering and living out the proper *telos* of humanity as revealed in Jesus Christ.

It is important for us to recognize that the role of Therapist may be acted out in formal counseling settings in the church, but it may also be more subtly dangerous in less obvious settings, such as preaching and fellowship. When preaching merely helps us to accept the world in its sin and does not call us to the reality of God's work among us that enables faithful living, then the Therapist has triumphed. When our fellowship is a "conspiracy of cordiality" (Hauerwas and Willimon 1989:138) rather than the communion of the reconciled, the Therapist has triumphed. These triumphs of the Therapist may lead to a growing congregation and apparent success, but they do not lead the Christian community into faithful living.

The third character that MacIntyre identifies in our culture is the Manager. If the Therapist and the Rich Aesthete represent roles in our private lives (as demarcated by our culture), the Manager governs our public lives. According to MacIntyre's analysis, the Manager may be the most pernicious of these characters. For a culture living out the consequences of the failure of the Enlightenment project, the Manager seeks to achieve maximum bureaucratic efficiency without regard to the end. Thus the Manager's authority is justified in our culture, first, by belief in "the existence of a domain of morally neutral fact about which the manager is to be expert." Second, the Manager is believed to know "law-like generalizations and their applications to particular cases derived from the study of this domain" (MacIntyre 1984:77).

The important point about the character of the Manager in our fragmented culture is that the Manager's effectiveness is thought to be morally neutral. That is, the Manager concentrates on mastering "techniques without any evaluation of the ends toward which the techniques are developed" (Jones 1995:40). Morality, then, is outside the realm of the Manager's competence and responsibility.

MacIntyre argues that this claim to managerial effectiveness is a "fictitious, but believed-in reality" that is central to our culture. For this reason, he devotes two important chapters to showing the illusory nature of our belief in the domain of morally neutral fact and the predictive power of generalizations in social science to which the Manager claims special access. In this critique, MacIntyre allows modest claims to managerial effectiveness, but disputes the larger claims to managerial power that so often mark our culture. The persistence of those larger claims and our acceptance of them, he shows, depend upon the moral fragmentation of our culture and the histrionic skills of the Manager (whom MacIntyre sometimes labels "the bureaucrat"): "The most effective manager is the best actor" (MacIntyre 1984:108). By this claim, MacIntyre means that despite the illusory basis of the Manager's claim to authority, that authority may be maintained by the Manager's ability to sustain the illusion by acting it out convincingly.

As the Western church participates in the consequences of the failure of the Enlightenment project, it may be infected by the character of the Manager. This infection may be difficult to diagnose, because we do not think of the church as a domain of morally neutral fact ruled by lawlike generalizations from the social sciences. However, in our morally fragmented world, the church may often find itself serving ends other than faithfulness to God. In this situation, the church may appear successful and the Manager may appear effective, but that success and effectiveness can be directed toward wrong ends.

Before continuing, we should note two qualifications. First, it is not success or effectiveness that is problematic. Rather the problem is that in our culture success and effectiveness are determined by the illusory convictions outlined above. Certainly, the church is called to be successful and effective, but it is called to be those things in relation to the mission given by God, not by our culture. Second, as I move on to criticize the church's use of the social sciences, that criticism is directed toward the practice of social science that is divorced from the question of ends and strives merely for maximum bureaucratic effectiveness.[21]

The church's capitulation to the authority of the Manager is tied to the centrality of that character in our culture and to the church's attempt to live with its history. Seeking to recover or to maintain our perceived place in the culture, we in the church turn to the Manager for guidance. So today, some of the most powerful leaders of the church are those who know how to manage public opinion and the political process in order to achieve success. If we examine the ends of that management, however, we may well question whether its success is directed toward making disciples.

Although the influence of the Church Growth Movement and its advocacy of the "homogeneous unit

principle" is fading, at one time this movement repre-
sented a powerful example of the authority of the
Manager. Drawing largely on social science, this movement argued that the most effective means for growing
churches was through targeting homogeneous units.
The social scientific apparatus that accompanied this
argument and its apparent effectiveness drew many
churches into its orbit. Today, most advocates of this
movement have greatly modified their position and
propose modest claims more in line with MacIntyre's
analysis of managerial effectiveness. Nevertheless, the
movement stands as a reminder of the church's capitulation to the character of the Manager.

Finally, drawing on MacIntyre's analysis of the character of the Manager, we can learn to be on guard against
the perpetuation of the authority of the Manager
through histrionics. In recent years, many sincere followers of Jesus Christ have been made captive to good
acting. What else are the televangelists but prime examples of MacIntyre's dictum that "the most effective
bureaucrat is the best actor?" Quite apart from these
highly visible Managers, many local churches aspire to
have pastors who differ from televangelists only in the
degree of acting ability they possess and in the private
morality they live out. That is, they do not see the pernicious effect of the Manager on the church's faithfulness. They want a pastor who combines managerial
effectiveness with private morality.

The Third Lesson

The Western church has lived through the failure of the
Enlightenment project in the culture and in its own life.
We now live with the consequences of that failure. As

MacIntyre warns us, that failure and its consequences are difficult to discern. Many good and wonderful things are entangled with much unfaithfulness. To exercise discernment and to recover faithful living will require effort by each of us—the exercise of the gifts of the Spirit in the body of Christ. So we turn in the next two chapters to what we might learn from MacIntyre for such discernment and faithfulness.

4

Recovering Tradition[22]

In Chapters 1 and 2 we considered what the church might learn from MacIntyre for living faithfully in a fragmented world by learning to live with our history. In Chapter 3 we considered what the church might learn from MacIntyre's narrative of the failure of the Enlightenment project and the consequences of that failure. In this and the concluding chapter, we will consider what the church might learn from a second story narrated by MacIntyre.

The Aristotelian Story

In *After Virtue*, MacIntyre develops his argument by telling two stories.[23] The first story, the failure of the Enlightenment project, has already given us a number of lessons. The second story that MacIntyre tells is of the classical tradition of morality. In telling this story, MacIntyre seeks to vindicate and recover a form of the Aristotelian moral tradition. MacIntyre's narrative of this tradition begins with the earliest Greek poets of heroic society and then moves on to the dramatists and philosophers of early Athenian society. After MacIntyre scrutinizes Aristotle's detailed account of this moral tradition, he considers the medieval "dialogue with"—rather than "simple assent to"—the Aristotelian moral tradition (MacIntyre 1984:165). MacIntyre argues that this dialogue brought three improvements to the classical moral tradition: (1) it recognized the inevitability of conflict and met conflict with the Christian virtues of charity and forgiveness, which were entirely missing in Aristotle; (2) its understanding of God's grace meant that neither Aristotle's *fortuna* (the bad luck of ugliness, low birth, childlessness, or other such circumstances) nor evil (provided we do not become complicit) excludes anyone from realizing the human good; (3) it incorporated a fuller understanding of human historicity. Aristotle understood that the moral life is lived in a particular place; the medieval thinkers recognized that the moral life is also lived within a particular history.

This is the moral tradition that the Enlightenment sought to escape. Now that we see the failure of the Enlightenment project, MacIntyre advocates a recovery of some form of the Aristotelian tradition. His constructive proposal consists of five elements: the conception of a practice, an account of the virtues, a narrative account of the good life (the *telos*) for a human, a living tradition, and a community within which these are set. MacIntyre spends several chapters developing and defending his proposal. He contrasts his position to competitors, defends it against objections, and argues for its viability, even its necessity.

A Revision of MacIntyre

MacIntyre's proposal provides us with several lessons for living faithfully in a fragmented world. However, before we turn to those lessons, we must consider a weakness in MacIntyre's proposal as it stands in *After Virtue*. MacIntyre has since revised and expanded his argument, most notably in *Whose Justice? Which Rationality?* Nevertheless, to make full use of his proposal for the church, we must revise it.[24]

The weakness in MacIntyre's account in *After Virtue* is that, although he advocates a recovery of the moral tradition, no specific moral tradition is present.[25] He argues for a conception of practices but advocates no specific practices. He argues for virtues but no particular virtues. His proposal, as it stands in *After Virtue*, is a torso without a head, onto which any number of heads may be grafted. John Rawls (1993:Pt. 3, Lec. 4), for example, has given an account of liberal democracy, the development of which is inextricably tied to the Enlightenment project that MacIntyre decries, as a tradition with practices and virtues set within a community.[26]

Thus MacIntyre's account in *After Virtue* must be revised. In part, I think this weakness is due to the fact that *After Virtue* represents a stage in MacIntyre's return to Christianity. As I have already noted, MacIntyre himself revises his account in later writing. Nevertheless, his account gives us some guidance for living faithfully in a fragmented world, to which we will add some theological substance.[27] Although the five elements of MacIntyre's proposal fit tightly together, for the sake of clarity we will consider them separately and then weave them back together.

Before turning to our constructive account, I must add one more caveat. If MacIntyre's account of our circumstances is generally accurate, as I believe it is, then this constructive account will lack initial plausibility because we are in a situation in which it has few exemplars. That

is, the real force of MacIntyre's constructive proposal
rests in its embodiment in the life of a community.
Lacking communities that exhibit such force, accounts
such as mine can only grope toward living faithfully. In
the end, it is not my account but faithful communities
that will teach us how to live faithfully in a fragmented
world. Nevertheless, drawing on MacIntyre's insights, we
may gain some understanding of what we are groping
toward, by God's grace.

The Good Life

In MacIntyre's account, he shows that our moral fragmentation largely results from the loss of the conception
of the *telos* of human life. Because this loss is at the heart
of our fragmentation, it is helpful to begin our constructive account at this point. In *After Virtue*, MacIntyre pro-
visionally defines the *telos,* or "good life," for humans, as
"the life spent in seeking for the good life for man"
(MacIntyre 1984:220). Although this conclusion is provi-
sional, MacIntyre gives little further explanation in *After
Virtue*. In spite of the rather abstract account MacIntyre
gives of the good life, he does make clear that we must
recover some notion of the *telos* of humanity.

The Christian notion of the human *telos* may be
described in various ways. In MacIntyre's later work, he
moves toward a more Christian and theological conception of the good life by drawing on Thomas Aquinas's
assertion that the human *telos* is "that state of perfect
happiness which is the contemplation of God in the
beatific vision" (MacIntyre 1988:192). In an earlier discussion, I drew on the Westminster Catechism's teaching
that the true end of humanity is "to glorify God and enjoy
him forever." We may add to this Paul's assertion that the

purpose of God's work is that "all of us come to the unity
of the faith and of the knowledge of the Son of God, to
maturity, to the measure of the full stature of Christ"
(Eph. 4:13). Although these statements use different language and images, they give compatible descriptions of
the human *telos* revealed in the gospel of Jesus Christ.[28]

The lesson for the church to learn from MacIntyre
is that we must revitalize our ability to give an account
of the good life for humans that is revealed in the
gospel. This revitalization will not end conflict; indeed,
it may heighten conflict. But at the same time, on
MacIntyre's account, it will enable us to locate those
conflicts properly. In so doing, it will also enable us to
live more faithfully by the gospel rather than the
Enlightenment project.

The most important lesson to learn from MacIntyre
about our attempts to give a Christian account of the
good life, is that we must learn to live and to think teleologically. That is, Christians must seek continually to
give an account of our lives that coheres with our *telos*.
In so doing, we can resist, and even overcome, the
moral fragmentation of our lives by continually seeking
to order our lives toward our conception of the human
telos. In other words, we must learn to give an account
not just of *what* Christians do, but also of why we do it
in relation to the conception of the human *telos*
revealed in the gospel.

This kind of living and thinking examines our practices to see if they are coherent with our understanding
of God's purposes for humanity. Take, for example, the
Church Growth Movement. Can we give an account of
how practicing the "homogeneous unit principle"
coheres with Paul's call to unity in Christ, which occurs

in the same letter in which he describes the crumbling of the wall between Jew and Gentile (Eph. 2)? Or consider our practices of forgiveness. Are they ordered toward therapeutic happiness, managerial control, or reconciliation in Christ? At all points in our lives, we must ask whether our lives are directed toward maturity in Christ or toward some other competing, and often unrecognized, *telos.*

MacIntyre, then, teaches us to think teleologically, to identify the human *telos* and order our lives toward it. Such ordering cannot be sustained alone; it requires the other elements of MacIntyre's proposal. Because, as noted above, the quest to identify the human *telos* may intensify rather than reduce conflict, we turn now to MacIntyre's account of this kind of conflict.

The Living Tradition

According to MacIntyre, a living tradition "is an historically extended, socially embodied argument, and an argument precisely in part about the goods which constitute that tradition" (MacIntyre 1984:222). In this description, MacIntyre acknowledges that teleological thinking brings conflict—precisely over the *telos* toward which our thinking should be ordered. But he also places that conflict within the large context of a "living tradition." It is the nature of the conflict and what counts as important in that conflict that constitutes a living tradition.

If we recover this understanding of living tradition for living faithfully in a fragmented world, we will begin to discern ways in which the church has been corrupted in Western culture. We will begin to recover arguments, like the ones noted above, over whether this or that practice of the church is oriented toward the proper end. We will also begin to argue about what constitutes that proper end.

In these arguments, we must learn from MacIntyre how to understand the "rationality" of tradition. First, we must learn what it means to participate in a *living* tradition. In MacIntyre's account, a living tradition may be conservative, but it is not static. Over time, tensions and contradictions may arise internally and externally. A living tradition responds to these tensions and contradictions in various ways. Some traditions decay over time and lose their potency; they "die." Others emerge from such challenges stronger than ever.

In Acts 15, we have a wonderful example of the church's participation in a living tradition. There the early church confronts an apparent contradiction: faith in Christ and the presence of the Holy Spirit have been given to uncircumcised Gentiles. These events are a profound challenge to the tradition of the church. Yet, as John Howard Yoder shows, they respond to this challenge from within the tradition and emerge faithful and strong (Yoder 1984). The conflict does not end, but it now takes place as a "socially embodied argument" about the goods—in particular, one good, circumcision— that constitute the tradition.

The second lesson we must learn from MacIntyre's account of a living tradition is the rationality of tradition over against other forms of rationality. In the work that follows *After Virtue,* MacIntyre devotes much energy to this topic (MacIntyre 1988:chap. 18; 1990). This topic is too complex to give a full account here. Suffice it to say that in the gospel the church not only has a living tradition but an ever-present reality. That is, the gospel is not merely something from the past that continues to live on in the memory of the church; it is also, and more significantly, the redeeming work of God in Jesus Christ present in the past and present today. The church's calling is to discern that present reality and live faithfully in it. Thus the life of the church embodies the rationality of the gospel.

In a church marked by the moral fragmentation of the Enlightenment project, such an outcome cannot occur. But in a church that is seeking to be faithful to a living tradition under the guidance of the Holy Spirit, such an outcome is promised. However, the existence of such a church depends upon further elements in MacIntyre's proposal.

Practices

In MacIntyre's proposal, "practice" takes on a very specific meaning. In a lengthy and complex description, MacIntyre defines a practice as

> any coherent and complex form of socially established cooperative human activity through which goods internal to that form of activity are realized in the course of trying to achieve those standards of excellence which are appropriate to, and partially definitive of, that form of activity, with the result that human powers to achieve excellence, and human conception of the goods involved, are systematically extended (MacIntyre 1984:187).

From the many things that we may learn from this definition for living faithfully, I will draw out three.[29]

First, we must simply learn to think of the church's activities as practices in MacIntyre's sense. Many, if not most, of the church's activities today lack this understanding of practice. We do many things as a church, but we would find it difficult to give an account of how those activities reflect our conception of the human good and how those activities constitute the church as a community.

For example, as I noted in an earlier chapter, the form and style of worship is a source of conflict in many churches today. It is often difficult to see this conflict as anything other than an expression of personal preference. If we formulated the conflict in terms of MacIntyre's practice, then we would better be able to locate the conflict appropriately in relation to the goods of the church and the enhancement of our ability to conceive and extend those goods. In this understanding of our conflicts over worship, "excellence" in worship would be defined in ways "appropriate to, and partially definitive of" the practice of worship, not of, say, group therapy, entertainment, or a motivational rally.

Second, we must learn from MacIntyre's notion of practice the importance of "internal goods." As noted in Chapter 2, in a morally fragmented culture we often orient our activities toward goods or ends that are external to that activity. In MacIntyre's account of practice, he exposes that mistake. Of course, a practice may lead to goods external to the practice, but the integrity of the practice as practice depends upon the achievement of goods internal to the practice.

To return to our previous example, someone may play basketball to achieve goods internal to basketball, such as physical exercise or camaraderie. Or one may play basketball for goods external to basketball, such as winning a college scholarship or achieving fame and fortune. In the first instance, basketball is a practice; in the second instance, it is not. Likewise, in the church we may engage in activities as practices, or we may transform our activities into something else. We may, for example, engage in evangelistic activities as a practice to achieve goods internal to that practice: attaining the unity of faith, full knowledge of Christ, and maturity as believers. Or we may transform those activities into something else by seeking to increase our "giving base," having the largest church in town, or increasing our reputation and influence in the denomination. If we learn from MacIntyre to think of the activities of the church as practices, then we will be better equipped to live faithfully in a fragmented world.

Third, we must learn from MacIntyre's conception of practice the need to extend our conception of the good and our powers to achieve that good. In other words, practice takes time and discipline. One of the mistakes of the Enlightenment is to think that moral action and moral community are simply the product of a decision to act morally. That is, in spite of my previous history of acting immorally, I can, in the moment, decide to act morally and actually do so. To be sure, the gospel teaches us that we who are sinners can, by God's grace, be made righteous. But there is also great emphasis on transformation, on growing toward maturity. In theological terms, we are sanctified by the work of the Holy Spirit.

MacIntyre's description of practice gives us an understanding of this process of growth in sanctification that illumines our circumstances so that we may live faithfully with our history as the church in Western culture. Faithful living is not achieved in a moment or through mastering technique. Rather, faithful living is a lifelong process of "practicing church," as we embody and extend the human *telos* revealed in the gospel and our powers to participate in that *telos*.[30]

Virtues

The virtues, according to MacIntyre, are

> to be understood as those dispositions which will
> not only sustain practices and enable us to achieve
> the goods internal to practices, but will also sustain
> us in the relevant kind of quest for the good, by
> enabling us to overcome the harms, dangers, temp-
> tations, and distractions which we will encounter,
> and which will furnish us with increasing self-
> knowledge and knowledge of the good (1984:219).

MacIntyre's retrieval of "virtue ethics" has received considerable scrutiny from Christian theologians and ethi-
cists. Because the language of virtue is almost entirely
missing from the New Testament, and because virtue
often, though not necessarily, tends to place undue
emphasis on human ability to achieve the good apart from
God's grace, the language of virtue needs to be transfigured
for the church's use (cf. Hauerwas 1975; Hauerwas and
Pinches 1997; McClendon 1986; Jones 1990).

Perhaps the most helpful way for the church to use
MacIntyre's proposal is to use the language of character,
habituation, and disposition. This language emphasizes
that our practices are best thought of, not as momentary
exercises of the will, but as activities that *pattern* our life
in discipleship to Jesus Christ (Jones 1990:110–112).
This patterning of our lives on the life of Jesus Christ
creates in believers the character and the habits that are
ordered toward our true *telos*.[31]

This language helps us attend to our history as we
seek to live faithfully. In contrast to an account of
Christian living that focuses on momentary obedience,

patterning our lives in Christ teaches us to live teleologically, with a view to where we are headed. As Paul
argues in Colossians 3, if our destiny is hidden in Christ,
then our lives here and now should be ordered toward
that future. At the same time, this emphasis on character also teaches us to attend to our past. When we come
to Christ, we come as people formed by many different
goods. Those habits that we have acquired through the
years undergo transformation through our discipleship
to Christ. We acquire new habits as we engage in the
practices of the church. If we do not recognize the force
of our prior history and habits, we can easily become
discouraged by our initial attempts at discipleship. In a
culture that prizes the "mastery of technique," we must
learn from MacIntyre to prize Christian discipleship as
the lifelong practice and acquisition of the character
that transforms our lives in Christ-likeness.

Community

In many ways this entire book is an argument, drawn
from MacIntyre, about the nature of the church as a
"community" in the context of a morally fragmented
society. Therefore, for the church to be a community,
we must learn to live with our history, in a morally fragmented culture, amid the failure of the Enlightenment
project. In order to do this, we must reclaim our understanding of the human *telos* revealed in the gospel, participate in the living tradition of Christian faith, and
embody that *telos* and that tradition in our practices and
virtues (character). From these assertions, we may draw
out three characteristics of the church as community.

First, the church must be a community that stands
over against the world for the sake of the world. Because

the church lives by a *telos* different from the various *teloi* of the world, if the church is living faithfully it simply will stand over against the world. However, because the church's *telos* is to witness to God's love for the world in Jesus Christ, the church's life is also for the sake of the world. In the many debates about the relationship between the church and the world, the import of this teleology is often missing. If the church is to be faithful to the gospel, it cannot do other than stand over against the world. Of course, even the faithful church will often look like the world. Our dress, our language, our architecture, our organization, and other elements will be drawn from our culture. But if we have a strong conception of the human good that is rooted in the gospel, then our use of these cultural elements will be significantly transformed. Moreover, to live faithfully the church must be explicit about its transformation of these elements for its own life and for its witness to the gospel.

Second, the church as a community must stand over against the world for the sake of the world. Because the church's conception of the human *telos* is a *telos* for all humanity, the church's faithfulness in living out that *telos* is the means by which the "world" may discover its true end and enter into the grace of God. In this way, then, the life of the church is given up for the salvation of the world just as Jesus Christ gave up his life for our salvation. In this way, the church preaches the gospel through a life lived over against the world.

Third, the church as a community lives by the grace of God. It is called into existence by the work of God the Holy Spirit. Once we were "not a people," but now we are "God's people" (1 Pet. 2:10). As God's people, we are called to point beyond ourselves. Our *telos* is not the survival and success of the church; rather, our *telos* lies beyond even the church:

> But the church cannot and will not preach this word unless it is ready, with true, yea, and fiery, evangelical zeal, to point beyond itself to the kingdom of God… [W]e can say, and we must say, that to join a church may provoke a hunger for a higher righteousness. It may create an awareness of the demand for a world-transcending loyalty, and it may open the eyes for the first time upon the possibilities of communion with God in Christ. We go about seeking those who for these ultimate reasons will identify themselves with those who love Christ and love in him all the sons and daughters of God (Hartt 1955:66).

These words of Julian Hartt anticipate in theological rhetoric the argument and the proposal made by MacIntyre in philosophical terms. By the grace of God given through faithful thinking and living, we may once again recover this passion for the gospel that is the very reason for our lives and for the church.

The Fourth Lesson

In his retrieval of the Aristotelian tradition, MacIntyre gives the church some directions for living faithfully in a fragmented world. That tradition needs considerable rethinking in the light of the gospel. This chapter has sought to begin that process, but it can ultimately be achieved only through the lives of faithful disciples who seek the human *telos,* the living tradition, the practices and virtues of the church, and the community that lives out Hartt's call to evangelical faithfulness.

5

The New Monasticism

In the concluding paragraph of *After Virtue*, MacIntyre expresses a clear-eyed pessimism and an enigmatic hope. Warning of drawing "too precise parallels between one historical period and another," he nevertheless draws on the waning days of the Roman Empire to suggest where we may be headed in Western culture. In that earlier time, he says,

> men and women of good will turned aside from the task of shoring up the Roman *imperium* and ceased to identify the continuation of civility and moral community with the maintenance of that *imperium*. What they set themselves to achieve instead—often not recognising fully what they were doing—was the construction of new forms of community within which the moral life could be sustained so that both morality and civility might survive the coming ages of barbarism and darkness. If my account of our moral condition is correct, we ought also to conclude that for some time now we too have reached that turning point. What

matters at this stage is the construction of local forms of community within which civility and the intellectual and moral life can be sustained through the new dark ages which are already upon us. And if the tradition of the virtues was able to survive the horrors of the last dark ages, we are not entirely without grounds for hope. This time however the barbarians are not waiting beyond the frontiers; they have already been governing us for quite some time. And it is our lack of consciousness of this that constitutes part of our predicament. We are waiting not for a Godot, but for another—doubtless very different— St. Benedict (1984:263).

I do not consider MacIntyre's pessimism to be misplaced. Indeed, the early chapters of this book are an attempt to show how the Western church is often ruled by the "new barbarians."

At the same time, I want to look with an even greater hope than MacIntyre expresses here for a "new monasticism" that will sustain, not the tradition of the virtues, but the witness to the gospel of Jesus Christ through faithful living. We can look with greater hope than MacIntyre expresses in *After Virtue* because we look to the power of God through the gospel to renew faithful living and witness. The new monasticism for which we look will be like the old monasticism in refusing both to shore up the *imperium* of contemporary society and to identify the future of civilization with the *imperium.* The new monasticism will be unlike the old monasticism because the history with which we live is a different history.

Because MacIntyre concludes his book with this

cryptic "prayer" for a new monasticism and leaves his
prayer undeveloped, the vision that I outline for a new
monasticism goes well beyond MacIntyre's book,
although it draws on his argument. Moreover, because I
am outlining a vision for what the church may be and
not a description of what the church already is, my
remarks here will be briefer than the previous chapters.
What I long for is not a new St. Benedict, but Christian
communities that may produce a new St. Benedict.
Before I outline that vision, we must first consider
MacIntyre's argument for a new monasticism.

Why a New Monasticism?

MacIntyre's call for a new monasticism that does not
seek to support or be supported by larger society turns
on his analysis of the attempts of the Jacobin clubs of
the eighteenth century and Thomas Cobbett in the
nineteenth century to retrieve the tradition of virtues
for the whole of society. As he demonstrates, these
attempts failed to achieve their goal; the Enlightenment
was so entrenched in larger society that it was, and is,
impossible to recover the tradition of the virtues for a
whole society. Drawing on the work of Jane Austen, he
shows that "both in her own time and afterwards, the
life of the virtues is necessarily afforded a very restricted
cultural and social place" (MacIntyre 1984:243).

What MacIntyre argues for the life of the virtues is
true in a different way for the life of the church. If my
critique of the life of the church in Western culture has
validity, then the only way for the church to recover
faithful living is for the church to disentangle its life
from the culture. That is, if the church is to recover
faithful living in Western culture, we must recognize the

restricted cultural and social sphere within which such a recovery will take place.

However, we must be very careful in describing our reason for disentangling the life of the church from the culture. We are not to withdraw from the culture because the culture is so bad that the church cannot be a part of it. The very mission of the church calls us to be in the world as witnesses of the redemptive power of the gospel. Nevertheless, there are times—and I have argued that this is one of them—when the life of the church has been so compromised that we no longer are capable of fulfilling faithfully our mission. At such a time, the church must withdraw into a new monasticism, not in order to avoid a "bad" society, but in order to recover faithful living and a renewed understanding of the church's mission.

This call to a new monasticism may sound irresponsible. Some will label such a vision "sectarian." We must recognize how much these responses depend upon the recent history of the church in Western culture. As I argued in Chapter 1, the church must learn to live with its history. In Western culture, the church has long been a force in the public arena. We have been taught to think of the church as the shaper of morality, the source of values. By thinking in this way, we have allowed the life of the church to be judged by the success and progress of civilization. So any suggestion that we withdraw from a role in shaping and guiding our culture appears to be an abandonment of the mission of the church. My argument here is that however well-meant this understanding of mission is, and however successful the church has been, it is a corruption of the church's mission and life. So, given this prevalent

understanding of the mission of the church and the corruption of the life of the church in Western culture, the
suggestion that we need a new monasticism will indeed
appear irresponsible and sectarian. However, if
MacIntyre's analysis and my development of it in the
previous chapters is correct, then for the sake of a lost
and dying world we desperately need the church to
recover a sense of its mission through faithful living.

The call for a new monasticism, then, is a contingent
tactic, necessary in this time and place for the church to
serve the world as God calls us to serve, not as the world
calls us.

Outline of a New Monasticism

Therefore we must hope, pray, and work for a new
monasticism that will, doubtless, be a very different
form of life. At least four characteristics will mark this
new monasticism. In some of these characteristics, the
new monasticism will be continuous with the old
monasticism; in other ways it will be discontinuous.
Because we have very few examples of this new monasticism, what follows is a vision of what I think we should
pray, hope, and work for, not a description of what we
already have. Doubtless, if some of the people of God set
to work on this vision, it will turn out very different from
what anyone may imagine at this point in our history.

First, the new monasticism will be marked by *a
recovery of the telos* of this world that is revealed in the
gospel of Jesus Christ. In recovering this *telos,* the new
monasticism will seek to heal the fragmentation of our
lives in this culture. Therefore, the new monasticism
will not be marked by a division between the secular
and the sacred. Rather, it will see the whole of life under

the Lordship of Jesus Christ. Such an understanding will not be achieved easily or quickly, but only through great commitment and struggle. The commitment and struggle necessary for a recovery of the gospel *telos* has little chance of occurring in the larger church. This task will be accomplished only in small, disciplined groups, in other words, in a new monastic movement.

Second, because this new monasticism will seek to heal the fragmentation of our culture, it will also be a monasticism *for the whole people of God.* That is, because it will not divide the world into the secular and the sacred, it will also not divide the people of God into religious and secular vocations. Rather, it will call all of the church to live faithfully by the *telos* of the gospel in the whole of life. Therefore, this monasticism may be lived out when a group of lawyers, teachers, business people, or others meet for lunch to consider together how their work may be ordered to the gospel. It may be lived out as families share their lives and resources with one another. It may be lived out as church leaders consider how to expel the rule of the new barbarians—the Rich Aesthetes, Managers, and Therapists—from the life of the church.

Third, because a renewed understanding of the human *telos* revealed in the gospel is not easily or quickly achieved, the new monasticism, like the old, will be *disciplined.* However, because this discipline will be for the whole people of God, it cannot simply be a recovery of the old monastic rules. Moreover, the monastic disciplines may be easily co-opted by the mindset of the Aesthete, the Manager, and the Therapist, so that they simply become a pleasurable experience, a managerial technique, or a way to achieve peace of mind. Therefore, the church must always be careful to orient its recovery of the disciplines of the Christian life toward its *telos*. The disciplines are a means to an end—the faithful life and witness of the church.[32]

Although the new monasticism must be intended for the whole people of God, the discipline that it requires will be achieved only through small groups of disciples that are themselves committed to the vision and discipline outlined here. As I indicated above, these small groups may be oriented around particular work or life circumstances. It may also be embodied in the church by a recovery of what Dietrich Bonhoeffer calls "the arcane discipline" (Bonhoeffer 1972:369–370). In his cryptic remarks, Bonhoeffer seems to be calling for precisely what MacIntyre suggests—a restricted space where the church protects its life from the corruption of the world so that it can truly become, once again, the church (Fowl and Jones 1991:155–157). In this arcane or "secret" discipline, the church restricts the celebration of the Eucharist to baptized believers. In this setting, the church may be more able to practice the mutual exhortation, correction, and reconciliation that marks a disciplined community.[33] Perhaps one of the reasons that the church in Western culture is not more disciplined in this sense is because of the "mixed" nature of the congregation that gathers for the Eucharist. In our emotivist culture, mutual exhortation and correction simply do not make sense. As a result, in most of the settings in which we celebrate the Eucharist there are powerful disincentives to the kind of discipline I am suggesting. If we are to recover faithful life and witness in the church, then in our culture we need to provide some restricted place in which the discipline of the church may be practiced. Of course, given the prevailing understanding and practice of baptism in the church, we may need to find other words to describe this restricted space.[34]

As we consider and practice this "discipline of the secret," we must also keep in mind that this separation from the world is not an abandonment of the world. Rather, it is a commitment by the church to be disciplined by the gospel for the sake of the world that God loves in Jesus Christ. Only in this way can the church live faithfully, witnessing to the gospel of Jesus Christ, which is the only hope and salvation of our fragmented world.

Fourth, the new monasticism will be undergirded by *deep theological reflection and commitment*. Only in this way can we remember the contingent, tactical purpose of the new monasticism. Here, MacIntyre's remarks may mislead us. In MacIntyre's account in *After Virtue*, the purpose of the old monasticism seems to be the provision of a place to maintain civility and the life of virtue. For the church, however, the purpose of the new monasticism is to provide the church with a means to recover its life and witness in the world. That is, the new monasticism is not a means of protecting our children from the world, nor is it a place to learn how to be civil so that society may one day recover civility. Rather, the new monasticism provides a means by which an undisciplined and unfaithful church may recover the discipline and faithfulness necessary for its mission in the world.

Therefore, by saying that the new monasticism must be undergirded by theological commitment and reflection, I am not saying that right theology will of itself produce a faithful church. A faithful church is marked by the faithful carrying out of the mission given to the church by God in Jesus Christ, but that mission can be

identified only by faithful theology. So, in the new
monasticism we must strive simultaneously for a recovery of right belief and right practice.[35]

Unanswered Questions

In the preceding section, I provide only the barest sketch
of a vision for a new monasticism. I am reticent to do
more, because I believe a new monasticism will take shape
through the gathering of committed disciples of Jesus
Christ. In other words, the new monasticism that we need
will not be the product of one person's vision; it will be the
product of the gifts of the Holy Spirit given through many
members of the body of Christ. As a result of this conviction, I have left many questions unanswered.

One unanswered question concerns the form of the
new monasticism. The old monasticism was separated
geographically, economically, and politically from the
larger society. This, of course, is an overgeneralization
that needs immediate qualification: the old monasticism
participated in many of the pressing issues of society.
Still, the question remains: How does the new monasticism separate its life from society? Should a new
monastic movement establish monasteries? Should it
somehow separate its economic life from that of society? I believe such questions can be answered only by
particular communities as they consider their callings
and their particular circumstances. I suspect that what
should develop is a mixture of forms, more and less separate from society. For example, I can imagine some
lawyers concluding that they can be followers of Jesus
Christ only by establishing their own practices. I can
imagine other lawyers concluding that they can indeed
follow Jesus Christ by practicing within a larger firm.

Likewise, I can imagine some establishing a new monasticism by intentionally living together and sharing a common life. I can imagine others living out a new monasticism without such arrangements.[36]

Other questions may also be left to the spiritual wisdom of particular communities and circumstances. What form should worship take? Should it be "high" church or "low" church? Should we seek to recover ancient liturgy? Should we practice the ancient monastic disciplines? What would the "simple" life look like today? These questions are vital, but I think that they are best answered in community.

As a new monastic movement considers these questions, three things must be kept in mind. First, even though they may be difficult to answer and may be divisive, such questions must be considered. Of course, we may conclude that considerable liberty should be offered in answer to a particular question, but that liberty must be the product of spiritual struggle, not easy capitulation to our fragmented, emotivist culture. Second, the answers that we give must be subordinated to the larger purpose of the new monasticism—the recovery of a faithful church. Third, our answers, I believe, should be placed within the context of the vision outlined above. That is, we must strive for a monasticism that does not separate the sacred and the secular, that does not distinguish among the vocations as to their ultimate *telos,* that forms disciplined communities, and that is rooted in deep theological commitment and reflection.

The Fifth Lesson

Although MacIntyre's remarks at the end of *After Virtue* are cryptic, they point the church toward the recovery of a new monasticism. This new monasticism exists today only in a few instances. In some places it is beginning to take shape. In other places it exists as a vision that has not yet been practiced.

Yet this new monasticism is what we are called to by my use of MacIntyre to analyze the life of the church in our fragmented culture. Given the history of the church in Western culture that I analyzed in Chapter 1, we are constantly tempted to form a church that will simply undergird the civil order. A new monasticism refuses that temptation. Given our fragmented world, the church is constantly tempted to import that fragmentation into its life. A new monasticism seeks to heal that fragmentation by rediscovering the *telos* of human life revealed in the gospel. Given the capitulation of the church to the Enlightenment project, and its consequent failure, the life of the church is constantly corrupted. A new monasticism seeks to practice a commitment and discipline that roots out that corruption and reforms the life of the church. Given the call to recovering tradition, the church needs a new form for its life that will seek and enable such a recovery. The new monasticism envisioned here is the form by which the church will recover its *telos,* the living tradition of the gospel, the practices and virtues that sustain that faithfulness, and the community marked by faithful living in a fragmented world.

I conclude with a prayer: God grant us your Spirit, that we may have the wisdom and power to live faithfully, and so to witness to the gospel of Jesus Christ, which is the only hope of the world.

Notes

1. Alasdair MacIntyre (1981; 2d ed., 1984). References to this book will be made to the second edition. Because my concern here is to draw on MacIntyre's work for the sake of the church's faithfulness to the gospel, I will seldom engage the secondary arguments about MacIntyre's work. For that discussion and further references, see the works by Horton and Mendus, Stout and Murphy, Nation, and Kallenberg in References Cited.

2. See the criticisms in Milbank (1990:326–379) and Hauerwas and Pinches 1997.

3. See, for example, Marsden (1994) and Van Braght (1950).

4. I will occasionally use "the kingdom" as a shorthand image for this ever-present reality of the gospel. For further development and defense of this notion, see Wilson 1996:chap. 3.

5. I do not have in mind here a similar-appearing approach that seeks to identify a thin thread of faithfulness in the history of the church. That approach is commendable as long as it does not confuse this "faithful remnant" with the kingdom or with the "only true believers." I will return to this later in the chapter.

6. For a fuller critique or Constantinianism, see Yoder 1984, Hauerwas and Willimon 1989, and Hauerwas 1990.

7. Although it is not the focus of this book, I should note that because of missionary activity and cultural expansion of the West, the history of the Western church includes the history of its impact on other cultures.

8. I do not make an argument for this assertion here. One of the main purposes of this book is to make an extended argument

for this assertion and for a more appropriate response to our situation that will enable the church to live faithfully.

9. I despair of finding a suitable term for what I am trying to describe. By "Western church" I mean those churches located in countries dominated by Western culture, mainly in Europe and North America, although New Zealand and Australia may be included, and many churches outside these geographical boundaries may be so "Western" as to be indistinguishable from the churches to which I refer.

10. MacIntyre's "disquieting suggestion" is presented at the beginning of his work as a hypothesis that depends for its force upon the extensive analysis that follows. I have chosen to follow MacIntyre's order of presentation here. If the reader is less than persuaded by this suggestion, I urge patience as the argument develops.

11. This characterization must be slightly qualified, because we in the West are encountering coherent outlooks in various schools of Islam and Asian traditions of Buddhism and Hinduism. This is one reason why these are so attractive to Westerners and why they present a significant challenge to the Western church. As part of the fragmentation of Western culture, the Western church often finds itself impotent in the face of challenges from coherent alternatives.

12. This claim is independent of the question of whether people remain within a tradition. The tradition and community may remain coherent even if people decide to leave it. Because many Muslims have only recently immigrated, how their communities and traditions contend with fragmentation remains to be seen.

13. I will further explore how to order our worship in Chapter 4.

14. There is a great deal more than this to learn from McIntyre's account of practices. We will return to this lesson in Chapter 4.

15. The cross is not merely a symbol; it is most importantly a historic event in the life of Jesus Christ that is our redemption. Nevertheless, today actual crosses are "fragmented symbols" in the sense that I am going to develop.

16. At present a number of theologians are seeking to reha-
bilitate Schleiermacher's work by overthrowing the traditional
reading that I present here. If they succeed, that will not
change the force of my argument here, which turns on how
Schleiermacher has been read. If he is "revised," then he will
become an exemplar of the position I am advocating.

17. That MacIntyre does not himself fully realize our situation is indicated by the fact that he continues to develop and
rewrite his arguments in his later works.

18. The best and fullest account of this process may be
found in McClendon and Smith 1994.

19. MacIntyre gives his account of these characters primarily in Chapter 3, "Emotivism: Social Content and Social
Context," and Chapter 6, "Some Consequences of the Failure
of the Enlightenment Project."

20. To be fair, we should note that not all therapists play out
the character of the Therapist as MacIntyre describes it.
However, given the power of a cultural ideal, we must also recognize how difficult it is to resist this role.

21. In a *tour de force*, John Milbank deconstructs theological reliance on social theory and relocates social questions
within ecclesiology in Milbank 1990.

22. Here we turn to MacIntyre's constructive counterpro-
posal to the Enlightenment project. This proposal could be
characterized in a number of ways, each of which has its limitations. I have chosen "tradition" as a way of faithfully reflect-
ing the development of MacIntyre's proposal beyond *After
Virtue* (MacIntyre 1988, 1990).

23. This and the following three paragraphs are adapted
from Wilson 1990:40–41.

24. Even with this later work, MacIntyre has still received
considerable criticism for his neglect of substantive theological
convictions (Jones 1990; Milbank 1990; Hauerwas and Pinches
1997). The major purpose of my revision of MacIntyre's proposal will be to give some theological direction.

25. Some of the material in this paragraph is adapted from
Wilson 1990:41.

26. MacIntyre himself later acknowledges the "tradition" of liberalism and subjects it to critique in MacIntyre 1988: chap. 17.

27. For the purposes of this book, my account here will be suggestive. I develop my suggestions more substantively in two further books, *Gospel Virtures: Practicing Faith, Hope, and Love in Uncertain Times* (Wilson 1998) and a work in progress, tentatively entitled, *Practicing Church.*

28. In our section below on "living tradition," we will consider further the arguments within the church over different accounts of the human *telos.*

29. For further reflection on Christian practices that draw on MacIntyre, see Tilley 1994; Jones 1990, 1995; Hauerwas 1990; McClendon 1986, 1994.

30. I recognize that my account of practice here is somewhat cryptic and abstract. That is necessarily so within the confines of this book. I hope to extend my account in *Practicing Church.* However, no matter how extensive an account one might give of Christian practice, such practice must ultimately take place in actual communities of believers.

31. As with my account of practice, I am aware here that my account of virtue or character remains somewhat cryptic and abstract. I remedy this in Wilson 1998, where I give an extensive account of the central Christian virtues of faith, hope, and love, and the practices that sustain those virtues.

32. Obviously, much more needs to be said here. In the present context, all that I can do is point to the work of two writers who are faithful guides to this recovery: Henri Nouwen and Eugene Peterson.

33. For further description of what such a community might look like, see Bonhoeffer 1954.

34. I am not thinking here of infant versus believer baptism as much as I am thinking of the disconnection between baptism and discipleship.

35. For work that helps guide the church in this direction, in addition to the works already cited, see Saliers 1994.

36. For an insightful description of a variety of communities that provide some models and lessons for a new monasticism, see Smith 1994.

References Cited

Bonhoeffer, Dietrich.—1972. *Letters and Papers from Prison*. Reginald Fuller et al. trans. Eberhard Bethge, ed. New York: Macmillan & Co.

———. 1954. *Life Together*. New York: Harper & Row.

Dyrness, William A. 1989. *How Does America Hear the Gospel?* Grand Rapids: Eerdmans.

Fowl, Stephen E., and L. Gregory Jones. 1991. *Reading in Communion: Scripture and Ethics in Christian Life*. Grand Rapids: Eerdmans.

Frei, Hans. 1968. *The Eclipse of Biblical Narrative: A Study in Eighteenth and Nineteenth Century Hermeneutics*. New Haven: Yale University Press.

———. 1992. *Types of Christian Theology*. New Haven: Yale University Press.

———. 1993. *Theology and Narrative*. New Haven: Yale University Press.

Hartt, Julian N. 1955. *Toward a Theology of Evangelism*. Nashville: Abingdon Press.

———. 1967. *A Christian Critique of American Culture: An Essay in Practical Theololgy*. New York: Harper & Row.

Hauerwas, Stanley. 1990. *After Christendom*. Nashville: Abingdon Press.

———. 1975. *Character and the Christian Life: A Study in Theological Ethics*. San Antonio: Trinity University Press.

Hauerwas, Stanley, and Charles Pinches. 1997. *Christians Among the Virtues: Theological Conversations with Ancient and Modern Ethics*. Notre Dame: University of Notre Dame Press.

Hauerwas, Stanley, and William H. Willimon. 1989. *Resident Aliens: Life in the Christian Colony.* Nashville: Abingdon Press.

Horton, John, and Susan Mendus. 1994. *After MacIntyre: Critical Perspectives on the Work of Alasdair MacIntyre.* Cambridge: Cambridge University Press.

Jones, L. Gregory. 1990. *Transformed Judgment: Toward a Trinitarian Account of the Moral Life.* Notre Dame: University of Notre Dame Press.

———. 1995. *Embodying Forgiveness: A Theological Analysis.* Grand Rapids: Eerdmans.

MacIntyre, Alasdair. 1984. *After Virtue: A Study in Moral Theory.* Notre Dame: University of Notre Dame Press. 2d ed. First published 1981.

———. 1988. *Whose Justice? Which Rationality?* Notre Dame: University of Notre Dame Press.

———. 1990. *Three Rival Versions of Moral Enquiry: Encyclopedia, Genealogy, and Tradition: Being Gifford Lectures Delivered in the University of Edinburgh in 1988.* Notre Dame: University of Notre Dame Press.

Marsden, George. 1994. *The Soul of the American University: From Protestant Establishment to Established Unbelief.* New York: Oxford University Press.

McClendon, James Wm., Jr. 1986. *Ethics: Systematic Theology.* Vol. 1. Nashville: Abingdon Press.

———. 1994. *Doctrine: Systematic Theology.* Vol. 2. Nashville: Abingdon Press.

McClendon, James Wm., Jr., and James M. Smith. 1994. *Convictions: Defusing Religious Relativism.* Valley Forge: Trinity Press International.

Milbank, John. 1990. *Theology and Social Theory: Beyond Secular Reason.* Oxford: Basil Blackwell.

Murphy, Nancey, Mark Nation, and Brad J. Kallenberg. 1997. *Virtues and Practices in the Christian Tradition: Christian Ethics after MacIntyre.* Harrisburg: Trinity Press International.

Newbigin, Lesslie. 1986. *Foolishness to the Greeks: The Gospel and Western Culture.* Grand Rapids: Eerdmans.

———. 1989. *The Gospel in a Pluralist Society.* Grand Rapids: Eerdmans.

———. 1991. *Truth to Tell: The Gospel as Public Truth*. Grand Rapids: Eerdmans.

Plantinga, Cornelius, Jr. 1995. *Not the Way It's Supposed to Be: A Breviary of Sin.* Grand Rapids: Eerdmans.

Rawls, John. 1993. *Political Liberalism.* New York: Columbia University Press.

Saliers, Don E. 1994. *Worship as Theology: Foretaste of Glory Divine.* Nashville: Abingdon Press.

Schuller, Robert. 1985. *Self-Esteem: The New Reformation.* Dallas: Word Books.

Smith, Luther E. 1994. *Intimacy and Mission: Intentional Community as Crucible for Radical Discipleship.* Scottdale: Herald Press.

Stout, Jeffrey, 1988. *Ethics After Babel: The Languages of Morals and Their Discontents*. Boston: Beacon Press.

Tilley, Terrence W. 1994. In Favor of a "Practical Theory of Religion": Montaigne and Pascal. Stanley Hauerwas et al., eds. *Theology Without Foundations: Religious Practice and the Future of Theological Truth*. Nashville: Abingdon Press. Pp. 49–74.

Van Braght, Thielman J. 1950. *The Bloody Theater or Martyrs Mirror of the Defenseless Christians.* Scottdale: Herald Press. Original edition. 1660.

Wilson, Jonathan R. 1990. Living Faithfully in a Fragmented World. *CRUX* 26:4:38–42.

———. 1996. *Theology as Cultural Critique: The Achievement of Julian Hartt.* Macon: Mercer University Press.

———. 1998. *Gospel Virtues: Practicing Faith, Hope, and Love in Uncertain Times.* Downers Grove: InterVarsity Press.

Yoder, John Howard. 1984. *The Priestly Kingdom: Social Ethics as Gospel.* Notre Dame: University of Notre Dame Press.